Dedicated in Loving Memory and Eternal Thanks to

HERMINE MECH ROETZEL
MINNIE ROETZEL HOGUE
MYRTLE D. PETTIT ROETZEL

(grandmother, aunt, and mother)

Contents

Foreword

I ALMOST DID not write this book. After forty-two years of academia I did not need another book as much as I needed rest. Ensconced in a comfortable retirement, in relatively good health, with other service opportunities calling, and with a host of younger scholars attending to the importance of the Great Depression, there was no need for me to venture into American history, a field in which I am a novice. But the more I reflected on my childhood farm experience in the Great Depression, and the more I sought to link that experience with the current scene, the more I realized how important it was to try to give voice to others like myself who experienced the Great Depression from the inside. With the near daily loss of my peers from that period and with the awareness that in a decade the voices of those inside that polar national moment will only be a whisper, I decided to offer my account of coming of age in the Great Depression.

In today's youth culture when anyone over forty is deemed irrelevant, there is a danger that a consideration of a "so yesterday" past might be considered a bore. But, I subscribe to the truth embedded in the threadbare trove that the culture that ignores its history is destined to repeat it.

One example may suffice. Unlike the political, social and religious culture that shaped me and others in the Great Depression, the anti-intellectualism infecting current political and religious discourse seems alien and even dangerous. While a healthy skepticism of all human ideology is laudable, my people with little formal education recognized that intellectual development through higher education offered the best possibility for escaping the clutches of poverty and engaging in public service. At some deep unarticulated level they also knew that education is the necessary foundation for the American democracy they revered and fought to preserve.

The trauma that the Great Depression imposed on ordinary folk touched every facet of our lives--our music, literature, art, institutions, politics, health, income, values, religion and life expectancy. In spite of that dark trauma, however, the hope for a brighter future remained and the story telling tradition of southern culture did much to keep hope alive for a better time ahead. Even at the risk of being deemed irrelevant my rendering, I hope, will encourage others to share their experience of that epochal national moment to preserve its valuable lessons for the future. My account hardly attempts to glorify or sugar coat that demanding and sometimes tainted past, but to recall a national moment when correction for social ills still seemed possible.

Embedded in this farm narrative, I hope, is an articulation of the ways that that life heightened our sensitivity to the way our human destiny was linked to that of our mother earth. My still vivid recall emphasizes the profound importance of women shaping the narrative of the Great Depression, an importance oft neglected. They were hardly mindless or passive drudges, but planners, dreamers, administrators, organizers, teachers, and pushers. My dedication singles out three women, Hermine Mech Roetzel, and Minnie Roetzel Hogue and Myrtle D. Pettit Roetzel—grandmother, aunt, and mother—for special thanks. Ordinary in many ways--uneducated, pious, simple, honest, hopeful, hard-working, and loving--all played key roles in my unfolding story. The singular importance of the immigrant cluster shaping that family story and its devotion to and defense of its new land was replicated then and still in millions of other families.

I freely recognize that no book is a solo operation. Without the encouragement, critical reading, and suggestions of a talented, trained, and passionate circle of readers this work would have never seen the light of day. The front line included trained classicist and respected colleague Professor (Emerita), Elizabeth Belfiore, and husband teacher, volunteer, smart, devoted public servant Peter. They led the cheering section from beginning to end. Then came Jan Shaw-Flamm, professional writer, former student and brilliant long time employee at Macalester College who was diligent, helpful, and encouraging. Linda Brooks prepared the photos of the appendix for publication. To Linda, a photo artist of national repute, my debt is incalculable. I can hardly find the proper words to properly thank beloved wife, Caroline Roetzel, retired teacher of English literature and school administrator. Her watchful eye poured over every page multiple times and her specific corrections and suggestions were invaluable. I offer special thanks also to Kate Krichtman who read portions of this manuscript to resident parents of a senior facility. Kate's elderly mother, now blind, was once an instructor of writing at the University where I taught. She and Kate's dad both also came of age in the Great Depression and offered reactions I will always treasure. A much broader circle of readers also included American historians of note Professors James Stewart, and Mary Wingerd, and biblical scholars of international repute like Professor (Emerita) Jouette Bassler. Dr. Warren Kendall also was a thoughtful and helpful reader. All read and offered welcome evaluations of portions of the manuscript. Special grateful thanks belongs to decorated artist, Lisa Roetzel, who sketched the image of Bud my teacher of mule ways when I was only a child and as later noted probably saved my life. Her sketch on this book's cover is a thoughtful likeness of this animal friend. I would be remiss if I did not offer generous thanks to Gretchen Wills of Page Publishing for her efficient, helpful, diligent, patient, and supportive work as mediator of this project. While it remained anonymous the editorial staff was outstanding as well.

To these persons named and others unnamed belongs whatever praise this work may receive. The flaws, warts and all, however, are my own and I freely own them. I am hopeful the circle of readers for the completed work will include many who also came of age in the Great Depression, their descendants, and casual readers, young and old, who seek a fuller understanding of the ways that epochal period still shapes our future.

Chapter 1

Circles of Care

MOST CRISIS ACCOUNTS come from adults who see the big picture, but the lens of the child focuses more narrowly, more personally, and often more honestly. While there is no shortage of books on the Great Depression, almost all focus on the adult experience, but my story is different.* Born in 1931, I had an entire childhood that was framed by that epochal moment. Memories of the sounds, sights, smells, sweat, and high and low moments are still as vivid as they were to the boy I was then. While I cannot become a child again to sketch the grandeur and misery of that once upon a time, I can still tap memories that linger, like the sounds, sights, odors, and scars that still instruct and are precious. This collection aims to recall some of the humanity gleaned and the life shaped from being a child of the soil in the Great Depression.

The genesis of my story is ancient. In the 1880s, a gaggle of German immigrant families—the Klotzes, Kohls, Müllers, Mechs, Schmidts, and Rötzels—settled halfway between the beautiful Ozark foothills and the White River delta near Russell, Arkansas, on what was a onetime Quapaw Indian campsite (see appendix for insert

---

* See Alison Collis Greene, *No Depression in Heaven: The Great Depression, the New Deal, and the Transformation of Religion in the Delta* (Oxford, New York: Oxford University Press, 2016), pp. 272–296.

picture of Quapaw artifacts from the farm).[*] Native Americans and German immigrants were there for a fresh start in a habitat whose full breast nursed its children with wild game, fish, nuts, mushrooms, berries, persimmons, poke salad, wild onions, and medicinal herbs. That rich wooded flatland that the immigrants cleared and tilled offered hard, unforgiving, dry gumbo clumps that scuffed bare feet and defined the settlers as clodhoppers, who were distinct from hill-billies. Into that setting, I was born and raised.

The nickname Toon hung and still hangs on me and requires some explanation. When I was born, three brothers had preceded me. A cousin midwife, Edith Dessing, delivered us all in the farm-house living room. Country doctor Emerson was then summoned to examine each of us and sign the birth certificate. With farmwife chores demanding attention, my recovering mother had to have help after my birth. Irish maternal grandma, Pettit, came to help, but when she left, a multitude of numbing tasks awaited. There was no electricity, no running water, no indoor toilets, no washing machine, and no gas stove to make meal preparations for six easier. No thirty-four-year-old woman could manage all of her household duties and care for a feisty boy and, seventeen months later, his sister, Wanda, nicknamed Titter because he could not enunciate *sister*. This young mother worked all day every day, 7 days a week, 365 days a year, and in spare moments, she cared for flowers in the yard or laid out a quilt to piece together and stitch into winter cover.[†]

She had to have help. There was no money for a nanny; Grandma Pettit returned to her home in Oil Trough twenty-five miles to the north on the White River. Grandma Roetzel lived next door, but she had to manage the farm full-time. In desperation Mom drafted ten-year brother Lavon to serve as our nanny. The two older brothers,

---

[*] See W. David Baird, *The Quapaw Indians: A History of the Downstream People* (Norman: University of Oklahoma Press, 1980).

[†] See attached picture in appendix of young married couple, Frank and Myrtle Roetzel, in final goodbye as Frank leaves for military duty in France in World War I.

fourteen and twelve, were old enough for field duty and thus were exempt from nursing care.

Lavon became a wonderful nanny, whom we revered until his death in 2003. He rocked us to sleep at night; put us down for naps; changed and washed our cloth diapers; washed, filled, and gave us our bottles; told us *Grimms' Fairy Tales,* sang lullabies to us, and introduced us to a fascinating story world. For amusement, he had us huff and puff like the big bad wolf threatening to blow the house down of the three little pigs. Later, he taught us our ABCs and multiplication tables and saved us from an angry, growling, attacking sow on our walk through her pasture. And without parental permission or knowledge, he taught us our first swear words. It was no accident that he was a model for sister Wanda, or Titter, and me. We knew his skimpy, boney lap was a safe place, and on that lap, we often cuddled.

Being the youngest of the four boys was rocky for me. Older brothers teased me to tears, laughed when they were successful, and then mocked me as "Cranky Tune." The Cranky dropped out as too burdensome, and Tune morphed into Toon. Parental scolding did not deter them. Toon became the tag that marked me and remains to this day in my birth family and hometown, Russell. It was the name I answered to and the only name I knew when I entered our one-room White School at five. Mrs. Emdee, the teacher, was skeptical that Toon was a real moniker and learned from nanny Lavon that Calvin was the name to be entered on the class role. As hurtful as the brothers' teasing was, my parents convinced me that crying was not shameful, that tears could mark memorable moments in coming of age and could be signs not of weakness but of love and joy. Big boys who can't cry are hardly big or manly, they claimed.

Those teasing older brothers did more, however, than tease; they nurtured, they taught me sports, they protected me, they aided me in need, and they became models of service and generosity. My oldest brother, Franklin, was like a second daddy. He bought me my first bicycle when I was a mere penniless twelve-year-old. While faraway in England with the Army Air Corps on sergeant's pay in World War II, he answered my pitiful request for a loan to purchase a used bike for $15. In what was my initial first-class letter came the great surprise. In it was stuffed a good portion of his monthly sergeant's pay, fifteen one-dollar bills. When he returned home from the war, he took me shopping and bought me a leather pilot's jacket. I was so proud. Later he would loan me his car for dates and be a model worthy of emulation. He gave himself unstintingly as a servant of public education and would become the primary caregiver of our aging parents and bachelor uncle Leo.

Another teaser, brother Leonard, was a strong and generous model. He excelled in all sports and hunting skills. He played *and* worked hard. He loved the lakes and ocean and always found a way to laugh even in life's low tides. His strength, generosity, good humor, and unfailing loyalty shape me to this day. It was he who warned me to refuse tobacco's lure if I wanted to do sports, and even though I was not much good at sports, that warning probably saved my life (five of our family died too early from tobacco-induced illnesses). Those teasing brothers who created the nickname Toon gave it special meaning and were a vital part of the family that nurtured me.

This circle of fraternal and parental care extended far beyond that immediate family cluster to include nearby kin. My immigrant grandmother was widowed at thirty when her young husband, Franz, and father of their four children died from two rattlesnake bites in rapid succession as he cleared a pathway. With no medical attention nearby, the poison was too much, and he left behind a widow after ten happy but short married years. Three of those children ultimately married and settled within a quarter mile of their mother. Bachelor uncle Leo never left home to marry and have a family of his own; he had once taken a chance on love, so the story went, but that didn't work out, and the hurt was so painful that he never took another chance. After Dad married Mom, they settled a quarter of a mile away. He and Uncle were a close-knit team until death. Grandma's daughter, Minnie, married a Dutchman, John Hogue, and settled a quarter of a mile on another side. The other daughter, Theresa, and her husband farmed a plot adjoining her land on the east, but they moved away before I knew them well. Each unit of my family remaining worked hard and supported each other in a world that was not always friendly. But the religious training Grandma had in the old country informed her love, faith, and guidance she offered to all. (See the copy of her Lutheran Confirmation attached.) None ever to my knowledge uttered a word of profanity. None gave any quarter to braggarts, "blowhards," or liars, and none succumbed to hatred or recrimination for petty slights. It was that circle of care that surrounded and nurtured me from birth.

The immediate family was primal, but the extended family also nurtured. First in the line of care was immigrant Grandma Roetzel,* who never learned to speak English. From her I came to understand German and most especially her command to Uncle to "krieg ein Kek für das Kind" ("fetch a cookie for the kid"). Her cookies made with fresh sorghum from a local plot still rank as the best I ever remember tasting. But more importantly, from her came my most vivid early experience of grace. The setting for that remembrance was of our family doing fieldwork for Uncle and Grandma on a hot, humid morning. As a child, I am sure I could not do much, but at the end of the day, I was given either a quarter or half dollar. At about eleven, we broke for early "dinner." Coming to Grandma's house sweaty and famished, we "washed up" and gathered around a table loaded with ham, liverwurst, mashed potatoes, gravy, green beans, sliced garden tomatoes, fresh oven-baked bread, and a luscious peach cobbler hot from the oven. Being famished from my attempt at a morning of work, I loaded my plate as the dishes passed; then I began silently and rapidly devouring that delicious fare with my spoon. Very soon I realized I had made a terrible mistake; I could not possibly consume all that my plate held. Even though I well knew and understood the adage "Waste not, want not" and the admonition "Eat what you take," I felt more ill with each bite; I knew if I ate it all, I would vomit. Grandma, sitting at my elbow, noticed my plight and the panic my face was showing; she gently, lovingly, and poignantly touched my elbow and whispered in German, "Du muss nicht Alles essen" ("You do not have to eat it all"). Then she made eye contact with my dad across the table and muttered, "Ruh" (quiet). Thus, she

---

*   See attached picture in appendix of twenty-year-old Hermine Mech Roetzel with husband, Franz, and newborn Leo (Leonhard) in 1886.

shielded me from his scolding. My relief was beyond words. I knew I had made a mistake, but her gentle touch and kind words eased my pain, erased my shame, gave me peace, and taught me the profound meaning of grace, even the grace of God. The leftover food from my plate went to the pigs and made them quite happy, I am sure. Years later I could come to realize that my understanding of the love of God was shaped by the unconditional love she showed.

Another memorable affirmation of worth came from aunt Minnie, Daddy's sister. One hot summer day in August, she walked from her house, a half mile away, through the pasture to our modest, unpainted, board-and-batten three-room farmhouse. She and my mother sat in the large entry room on red-oak straight chairs, chattering away. I stood next to her, eavesdropping on their animated conversation. Suddenly she grabbed me, plopped me on her copious lap, hugged me, kissed my cheek, and whispered in my ear, "Happy fourth birthday." She was the first that I can remember who ever give me a birthday wish, and that was one of the most precious birthday presents ever. With a farm family of seven in desperate need and the Arkansas per capita income in the drought year of 1935 of only $191, all of our collective energy was devoted to surviving; there simply was no time or money to mark all of those special occasions. Aunt Minnie, however, took the time to interrupt her work to walk a half mile to celebrate my existence with a hug and a kiss. Her expression of genuine love meant so much that seventeen years later, I would interrupt my seminary education to travel by train over three hundred miles to drive her home from the hospital where she lay dying of stage four cancer. I did so to honor her request to die at home. It is as clear as yesterday. I drove her home in Uncle John's newish Buick while he sat in the back seat with his long arm around her for what they both knew was her last trip home. Two short weeks later, I returned for her funeral. She was gone. To this day, small brass plaques attached to the church pulpit, communion table, and baptismal font beautifully crafted by Uncle John keep her memory alive.

When I returned to my seminary classes after the funeral, an eccentric nameless professor walked to my front-row classroom chair, pointed at my black suede shoes, and declared repeatedly, "Your feet are dirty. Look at them. Look at them. They are dirty." He used my dirty shoes to make the point that even, or especially, ministerial students have dirty feet—i.e., that we were all sinners. His assertion, of course, was correct. Only too well could we recite the line from the gospel song, "False and full of sin I am," when we needed instead to heed the line "Thou art full of truth and grace." When I later came to his office to admit that both metaphorically and literally, my shoes *were* dirty, I wanted to explain that they were dirty because I had just come from a grave. His abject apology salved my wound, but the memory of his shaming action still hurts.

Now I realize that the extended family that nurtured me included our farmyard animals. Our barnyard adjoined the lot encircling the house; that special proximity offered proof of our kinship with the barn creatures. That shared space made a point now taken for granted—i.e., animals and humans share the ability to empathize, love, affirm kinship, and mourn loss. Losing a dog, for example, like Black Lab and Dr. Tiberius—or Ti-Ti for short—was like losing a member of a family. Now, we better understand how animals have emotional transactions similar to those of humans. That knowledge was foundational for me as a child. Here I take note of only three members of that extended circle of care that nurtured me—a mule, Bud; a calf, Dickie; and a dog, Rack.

When all of my brothers went off to combat in World War II, I was eleven, and my responsibilities expanded to fill the gap left by their departure. A major responsibility that fell to me was animal care. Because I fed them, those creatures decided I was their friend. Our oldest mule, Bud, and I had a special friendship. He knew how to manipulate the gullible kid feeding him; he recognized that a friendly nose nudge would ask, "Aren't you forgetting something?" and thus would earn an extra ear of corn. Even after we were able to use my Uncle's Model A John Deere tractor and receive permission during the war for a model B, our mule team, Bud and Tom, was the instrument of choice for delicate plowing and harvest chores in which only verbal commands sufficed. Dad so trusted that team that he would send them out with me to plow strawberries, corn, cotton or potatoes. I soon learned to harness, pet, and direct the team through tricky maneuvers, hoisting huge fork loads of hay to the peak of the barn and then by rail to an ideal dumping place in the barn loft. The elder Bud was especially affectionate and fully obedient to my boyish verbal commands; it was almost as if he realized he had a responsibility to care for the little greenhorn I was. After feeding I always paused a bit to rub his nose and pat him on the side. Never in my years of working with him did he bite, kick, or lay ears back to threaten me. Though I weighed less than a hundred pounds and he weighed ten times that, he treated me as a kindred soul. In one case, that affectionate relationship may have saved my life.*

While tilling the strawberries with a cultivator pulled by Bud and Tom, the leather reins ran under my arms and knotted behind my back. That knot left both hands free to guide the plows, and on one warm, sultry summer day, we were plowing, and my eyes were so fixed on the ground that I did not notice the dark cloud blocking the sun. As we plodded along, my stupor was shattered by a sudden blinding flash of lightning followed immediately by deafening thunder. The mules, whose small hoofs were clad with iron, misnamed "*horse*shoes," felt the shock of the lightning strike and panicked. They ran and dragged me headlong behind the cultivator down the furrow. Had my head collided with a rock or a stump, I could have been paralyzed or killed. Panic-stricken, I screamed "Whoa, whoa, whoa" at the top of my voice. Sensing my panic and in spite of his fright, Bud slowed and brought his younger, more rambunctious teammate Tom to a halt. I then did the only thing I knew to do. Still shaking from terror, I walked to the front of the team and gently stroked Bud's nose; he wagged his head up and down nervously and knowingly. As time passed and the war seemed to be ending, Bud died, and his body was dragged and left in the distant corner of our farm woods. My grief was deep and lasting. He was not just a mule; he was a family member who cared for me. Not all persons enjoy such relationships. If abused, mules, like humans, can retaliate with kicks and bites, and when endeared, they can assume responsibility

---

*   See attached drawing of Bud in appendix.

for vulnerable children. As my teacher, he held the senior position and was my mentor.

Another member of the circle of care nurturing me was Dickie, a young calf. When chased by other animals in the pasture, a pregnant yearling had a premature birth. The calf was so premature that it did not yet have hair, and the doting mother's rough tongue licks caused it to bleed. Seeing its plight and knowing it would not survive if left with its mother, we took the calf into the house to feed it, care for it, and save its life. The calf became a household pet we named Dickie; I fed him bottles of milk and assisted with the house training. He not only survived but grew into a robust calf with special freedoms other calves never had. He freely roamed the premises and grazed and responded to my calls to come home for his evening feeding, petting, and bathing. As he grew, Dickie allowed me to ride him home at day's end until one day he decided I was a burden, and while crossing a bridge over a branch, he dumped me into the stream. It seemed like a playful joke, but he taught me a lesson. In Dickie I invested much, and he, like a dear soul mate, tolerated my colossal ignorance of calf ways and gestures. Like other young calves we raised, Dickie reached an ideal marketing weight, and I still remember the profound sadness I felt as Dickie was herded into the buyer's truck to be hauled away to market. I followed him beside the truck and can still remember the confused, terrified look on his brow showing through the truck's railing. When the truck drove away, I was devastated. To mollify me, Daddy gave me the $13 he received for Dickie, but that only added to my woe. How could I spend the money paid for one so precious? It would have been a sacrilege to splurge it on treats, ice cream, movies, clothes, or carnival rides; the decision weighed *so* heavily. Months later and in agony, I decided to spend the money on my first trip to dentist Dr. Gill in Judsonia, ten miles away. My thirteen fillings and the removal of two upper impacted wisdom teeth took it all. The cost might have been higher had not Dr. Gill factored in the story of my loss that I shared with him. At least I gained some comfort from knowing that my first-ever fillings offered direct connections to that beloved animal. Now over seventy years later, I always remember

Dickie when I go to the dentist as I did just the week I crafted this memory token (June 5, 2017).

Rack, our dog, knew his place also as a family member. He ate the scraps from the table, slept under the house, and as our senior, was especially protective of sister Wanda and me. He needed no order to lead us on our blackberry-picking jaunts or to explore briar patches, clearing them of rattlesnakes and copperheads for our berry-picking ventures. That dog relationship was dear to us and was unique *and* affirming. Even when our naughtiness merited a parental scold, Rack would always unconditionally accept us, take our side, affectionately lick our hands and face, and be glad for our presence and petting. We had other dogs later, but none could ever take Rack's place or nurture and protect us as did he. It was a cruel injustice that the dog that protected us from rattlesnakes, copperheads, and water moccasins would die of a rattlesnake bite. The lives of these friends were nurturing and affirming; I mourned their deaths as keenly as did I that of persons.

From these experiences, I gained my respect and even reverence for animal life. That reverence, however, was hardly conflict-free. For the variety in our farm diet was provided by game hunted and taken in the surroundings. To celebrate this family hunting habit, I was once given an air rifle, or BB gun, for a Christmas present. I practiced using it and developed some skill at hitting the bull's-eye on my cardboard target. When I decided to really hunt, I chose a live target. By our corncrib, there were always loose grains or bits of corn eagerly sought by the sparrows and blue jays. That I chose as my first hunting ground. Peeking and sneaking around the corner of the crib, I spotted a small flock of sparrows devouring the spill. It was a sublimely happy scene with much chirping and scratching. I took careful and deliberate aim and slowly squeezed the trigger. A sparrow fell to the ground. Immediately I regretted what I had done. I laid the BB down, picked up the sparrow with my two hands, and saw its tiny bloodied body. I opened its beak and blew into its mouth, but there was no response. The sparrow was dead. I had taken its life; I had taken something that I could not give. My guilt was heavy, and that experience shaped me for life. Thereafter, as I matured, I had some limited hunting experience, but there was no joy in it. As my parents died, some of the farm guns came to me—a repeater .22 rifle with a scope, my first real gun; a 410-gauge single shot; and a Long Tom 32-inch 12-gauge shotgun. In 1963, after Kennedy's assassination, I could not bear to ever fire them again. I gave them away.

As a chaplain in the Air Force, I was required to practice firing a pistol, and I could hit the target, and sometimes I hit the bull's-eye, but I made it clear that I would never, ever fire a gun at an attacker. The lesson learned from my sparrow experience remained. Yet it was more than that experience that schooled me; it was the deeply personal relationships I enjoyed on the farm with other living creatures. To some that will sound like sentimental or even romanticized fiction, and that may be so, but if so, it is a fiction enfolding a truth. I endorsed the sentiment I only later came to know through the beautiful poem of Rainer Maria Rilke:

> Gladly do I hearken to Things singing.
> Touch them—How stiff and mute they are!
> You kill all my things.

Similarly, my childhood farm experience taught me a reverence for creatures that I could not view as "things" or as lifeless objects to be used and discarded.

The narrative I have sketched here was most aptly summarized by the novelist Lawrence Durrell in one of his novels: "We are children of our landscape; it dictates behavior and even thought is the measure to which we are responsive to it." Our tie to our landscape challenges the individualism of our time. We all, I suggest, rest on the shoulders of others—family (immediate and extended), teachers, friends, and ancestors now gone but still alive in our hearts. This recognition tends to dampen the almost universal tendency to take credit for our achievements, to elevate ourselves over others, to exclude and divide, and to disregard our debt and our responsibility to share where we can. Difference may open up to us worlds and visions that enrich and nourish. Otherness, however, when malevolently used, assigns an inferior or subhuman status to all other creatures that is bigoted and ugly.

In the pages below, I try to construct my memory's portrait of being a child in the Great Depression. I do not wish to glorify or romanticize that experience but to recall how the intelligence, character, imagination, grit, and love of an extended second-generation immigrant family caught in the trammel of the Great Depression all collaborated to make fulfillment possible for others. Depression families were poor not because they were stupid, lazy, unimaginative, careless, or even victims of an inborn mind-set as modern politicians sometimes suggest, but because of a very difficult hand of cards life dealt them and a complex web of other factors like terminal illness or tragic accidents. In a sense, a society that refuses to take note of or help its vulnerable is hardly civilized. In the pages below, I shall seek to recover aspects of my legacy—the stories that were memory keepers, the work demanded, the surprise visits that relieved, the play that renewed and refreshed, the homecoming of brothers who went off to war, the edginess I felt when leaving that spiritual landscape, and a brief summary of where it all led. Finally, I will report on my lifetime journey and how the three phases of my journey merged into one at the end. The words below offer a token of how lasting and life shaping the Depression was and how vivid its recall still is.

Sounds Music

I can still hear the sounds heard by the young boy I used to be.
The whip-o-will wafting across the meadow,
The cheep, cheep of sparrows scratching for food,
The soft coo of the dove in the barn lot with her mate,
The harumph of the frog bleating from the pond's edge,
The caw of the crow launching sparrow flocks,
The honk honk of geese off to warmer climes,
And the quack, quack of ducks talking on the pond.
Oh mother nature. Your music is sweet; it still warms my soul.

Chapter 2

Stories as Memory Keepers

HOURS BEFORE SOCRATES was to drink from the poisoned cup, he reflected on the afterlife with his students in the Athens agora: "The soul," he offered, "takes nothing with it as it enters Hades except what it has learned [*paideias*] and the life it has led" (Phaedo, 107D). When I was a junior in Hendrix College and enrolled in a philosophy course, I first learned how that important insight and inspiration is best understood when wrapped in Plato's story of the martyrdom of Socrates. Similarly, we also best understand the special cadence of Jesus's words, "Father forgive them," when wrapped in the story of his crucifixion. Likewise, the words "I have a dream" demand the Martin Luther King Jr. narrative and martyrdom for their poignancy. That symbiotic relationship between story and memory permeated every fiber of my being during my childhood in the Great Depression.

While they were down-to-earth, practical peasants, Myrtle and Frank Roetzel were also backwoods humanists. Neighbors often gathered on a Sunday afternoon on our unpainted farmhouse porch or that of Grandma and Uncle nearby. The image of those gatherings is as clear now as it was to the boy I was then. The men in their Tuf Nut overalls and blue denim work shirts sat on the porch, chewed Cotton Boll Twist tobacco, spat, whittled, smoked Prince Albert roll-em' cigarettes, and told stories. The women gathered inside to sip coffee, dip Garrett snuff, gossip, laugh, and tell their stories. Their stories linked their present to a past and imaged a future. There between the cotton field and apple orchard, those storytellers held a colloquium on the humanities. As a preadolescent, I transgressed with impunity the boundaries between those gendered worlds. I heard stories—great stories; sad stories; happy stories; stories of bravery and cowardice, success and failure, tears and laughter, hope and despair; stories of the triumph and failure of the little people and the humiliation of the proud. The witty surprises lacing those stories set off waves of laughter and left me leaning forward in suspense, reflecting on what-ifs, and hoping for future deliverance. Later I learned how those stories entertained, but they did more; they sustained and recalled important moments of the past and instructed a simple country folk for the future. They entertained and provided relief from work's burden. They reinforced core values, lightened the weight of inferiority's curse, tutored the imagination, comforted the distressed and hopeless, and sometimes reinforced dark prejudice.

Immersion in that story world may best explain why my later career would focus on the construction and interpretation of the stories of ancient peoples. I am now more aware of how that childhood cultural genealogy informed my scholarship and career of college and university teaching and made that vocation joyful. The story world of my youth heightened my sensitivity to the form and function of narrative in ancient cultures. It sharpened my sensitivity to the power and influence of stories in the ancient Near East, when over five thousand years ago, the Sumerians of the lower Tigris/Euphrates valley developed carved clay tablets then baked them to record business transactions in cuneiform *and* to recall *stories* that shaped their identity and habits of being. Stories like the Gilgamesh epic and Enuma Elish still offer insight into their sense of human origin and purpose *and* the special wisdom they gained from a heroic acceptance of one's mortality. The Arkansas stories I recall were certainly less profound but no less important in life's quest for meaning and inner peace.

1. Extended Family Stories

I well remember a Sunday-afternoon gathering on the hallway porch of Grandma's house and that of bachelor uncle Leo, whom we

addressed only as Uncle. At one end of the breezeway sat the octoge-
narian Uncle Jake, now blind but still mentally acute. Next to him
sat his son, Otto; then my Uncle Leo; Fred Dessing, a cousin by marriage; my dad; and then three neighbors. The elder Uncle Jake controlled the conversation with simple requests and questions requiring
answers. He loved funny and sad stories like the legendary one of
young boys Daddy and Uncle being sent off to the White River bottoms to check on the free-range animals. An unseen prankster neighbor with a sick sense of humor terrified those kids with a pale imitation of a panther's plaintive cry. In total fright, the young boys fled
for their lives. Uncle, my dad's six-year senior, raced ahead on foot as
Daddy followed on horseback, screaming, "Wait . . . wait . . . wait!"
Peals of laughter would always erupt, but that trick once stoked anger
and a stern warning from a relative.

Uncle Jake, a bit ashamed when the laughter came at the expense
of those onetime youngsters now sitting on the porch, sought to
underscore the importance of another singular and heroic moment
in their lives. Over the head of Uncle Jake hung two five-inch white
wild boar's tusks. Though he was blind, in his mind's eye, he could
still see those awesome teeth, and that reminiscence prompted the
question, "Leo, after all of these years, have you ever had nightmares
about the tusk event?" Uncle seemed to welcome the question and
began to tell how they hung there as a vivid reminder of the scariest
moment of his life.

He recalled how Grandma sent him (fourteen) and my dad
(eight) into "the bottoms" to break the ice on Horseshoe Lake to
provide drinking water for their cattle wintering there. After completing that task and returning home, they suddenly came face-to-
face with a roaring, charging wild boar. Instinctively, they fled, but
both knew they could not outrun that angry beast. In desperation
they sprang onto a large stump, and the boar followed, growling,
shaking his head, and snapping at their feet. The panic-stricken boys
were trapped. As the wild boar reared onto the stump, he roared,
shook his head, and opened his tusk-filled mouth to make a final
lunge. Uncle noted, "I was scierd to death, my heart was a-poundin',
and Frank was a-cryin'. I took my one last chance. I lowered my sin-

gle-shot, short-barrel 30-06 and pulled the trigger and luckily hit the boar right between the eyes. He crumbled and fell at our feet, and I just stood there a-shakin'. After we calmed down, we pounded out those tusks with the butt of the gun to provide proof of our defense, for no one would believe our story without evidence. When we told Mamma the story and showed her the tusks, she hugged us and cried. Through her tears, she muttered, 'I cannot imagine what I would have done if I would have lost you two after losing Dad just yesterday.'" (Really four years had already passed since husband, Franz, died from the double rattlesnake bite, but the pain was still as fresh as yesterday.)

After Uncle told the story, Uncle Jake posed *the* key what-if question. "What would've happened, Leo, if you had missed the boar's shakin' head? Would we ever have found your bones? How could Minnie have tilled the farm without you two feisty brats?" I listened closely, and at each telling of the story, I was terrified and wondered, *Suppose Uncle* would *have missed or only have wounded the boar, making him more angry and dangerous.* Uncle reported that he had three more cartridges, but they would have been useless, for there would have been no time to reload his single-shot rifle. Could Daddy have escaped up a tree after the boar killed and set about devouring Uncle? What if the boar would have killed them both? With a shock, I pondered this question. The question of *my* existence would have been moot. I still image how different *the* world would have been without these two children of immigrant parents. Second generation, now they were eager to prove they were real "'Mericans"; so also Grandma, who in 1916 changed their names so they would no longer sound so German and could go unnoticed.

In spite of her best efforts, though, on the eve of World War I, hostility toward German immigrants was as ugly in Arkansas as it was in Minnesota and New York. It was sometimes violent, brutal, and insulting and always demeaning. I had to ask my dad what being called a Kraut meant. On the eve of World War I, to prove their loyalty to the US, she initiated name changes. Grandma's German Hermine (feminine of Hermann) became Minnie, and her former husband, Franz, became Frank. The Leonhardt of Uncle became Leo.

And Daddy's baptized Franz Emil Daniel Roetzel became Frank E. Roetzel. Neighbors followed her example. Schmidts became Smiths, Müllers became Millers, Sister Adelaide became Addie, and Uncle Jacob became Uncle Jake. And though German was Grandma's first language until her death sixty years later, her children always responded to her in English.

To further prove, if proof were needed, his Americanization, Daddy went off in the fall of 1917 to fight the Germans in France. His three sons also all saw combat in World War II at Normandy, Iwo Jima, and Saipan. I later served as an Air Force chaplain riding the DEW Line with Alaskan bush pilots to serve airmen manning a string of radar stations across Alaska, Canada, and Greenland to warn of any potential Russian attack coming across the Arctic. Now it seems ironic that those immigrants once scorned put their lives at risk for the new homeland. The Union army in the Civil War had a German-speaking unit fighting for the emancipation of slaves from their white owners' control. One can now multiply that experience by millions and wonder what life in this country would have been like without my immigrant family and others like them.

Somehow now, with the deaths of all in that porch circle, the tusks have gone missing, and the story has fallen silent. Without the story, the tusks have no meaning. That is too bad, for they symbolized something terribly important about the human prospect, and they somehow signaled the life-forming act of storytelling.

As I left the circle, recounting stories of the wild boar, panthers, wolves, coyotes, mountain lions, and black bear, I sneaked into a more promising, lighthearted exchange of the women inside the house. I can still hear the recitations of the skimpy news from back "home"—i.e., family and friends back in Pomerania. "So and so is now dead," and "Oh, the once little Emma is now a grandma!" "Little Friedrich is a grandpa," etc. "Did you see the letter from Friedericke that was going around?" These friends and relatives, though distant, were not forgotten. Interestingly, after World War II, the German family and friends left behind received CARE Packages from these and other American families.

Those little comments would inspire Gram to interject her story about the pain she felt long ago when she, then eighteen, her mother, and six siblings boarded the train in Klein Machow, Pommern (Pomerania, see attached picture of countryside) to journey to the port and take passage to New York from Bremen in 1884 and then by train from New York City to Russell, Arkansas. She told of waving goodbye through tears to weeping friends and family whom she would never ever see again. The train would pass the church where she was baptized and confirmed (see attached picture) and by the cemetery where the bodies of relatives and friends rested; the recall of those sites set off more tears. Gram rehearsed the pain of that parting and the agony of days traveling third class in the belly of the ship and then the utter despair she and her mom felt when they discovered that some evil soul had ripped open their feather comforter (*Federdecken*) to steal their pouch of gold coin from the sale of their small farm in Pomerania. Seeking relief from that tortured, absorbing story, Aunt Addie, her sister, interjected in German, "Vielleicht wir sollten da noch wohnen" ("Maybe we should have stayed"). But Gram, who had already suffered much, would have none of it; she just exploded with denials—half in broken English and half in German spoken so rapidly, I could not understand. The strength of her denial with shaking hands and the tone of the remarks made it clear even to the non-German speakers (like my poor outsider Irish mother and this eavesdropping child) how even the trauma of tragedies in this new land had not dimmed the luster and joy of this new beginning. Grandma was no sentimental romantic; she was a realist, and she was proud of her parents for taking the chance they did when they would not live to see its fruit. She loved being able here to have her own land, to marry whom she loved, to raise her own grapes from seeds brought from Germany, and to make her own wine even though, in doing so, she violated Prohibition laws. This new circle of family and friends was now home and offered support and opportunity she would never have imagined in Germany. Even as a child, I felt proud and glad to be there on that hot, sultry, Sunday afternoon, playing with the cats and listening in on stories that transported, thrilled, and entertained.

Titter and I came to know who we were through this shared family narrative of collective stories. Those accounts taught us that expressions of a generous love gave life a luster even when hardship was numbing and demands for sacrifice overwhelming. The mega story of the early deaths of both maternal and paternal grandfathers recalled the sacrifice those accidents imposed on our parents when they were small children. Other stories intervened to lift the eyes up to a transcendent generosity.

2. Immediate Family Stories

Speaking of generosity, I think of the oft-recited story my brothers told of the stock market crash of October 30, 1929, and its aftermath in 1930 when over a hundred of Arkansas banks failed. Franklin and Leonard were just twelve and seven when the story began. They joined Daddy on a bumpy mule-drawn wagon trip to Bradford, our nearest small town with a bank. They arrived there, however, to learn that the bank in which Daddy had a small account had failed, and he was unable to draw money from that account for groceries. Undefeated, he assured the boys that he had another bank account in Bald Knob ten miles in the opposite direction; they would go there. They dutifully started the bouncy wagon ride, only to learn halfway there in Russell that the bank in Bald Knob had failed also. With just thirty-five cents in his pocket, my dad spent it all on candy for the boys and headed home. Obviously, they had some money hidden in the farmhouse, and Grandma and Uncle helped, and having no loans from the bank outstanding, they kept their farm when many of their neighbors lost theirs.

That story of my dad's reckless generosity dominated the family ethos our whole lives, sanctified the hard work that sustained, and offered celebratory occasions. Mealtimes especially offered delicious foods for sustenance and escape from the pain of backbreaking work and disappointments. The priestess of this ritual of escape was Mama, who did not always endorse Dad's generosity. Outwardly soured by the hand that nature had dealt her, she rejoiced in the control *her* kitchen gave in managing the Depression's deprivations. The list of her duties was long. Her labors were the force that gave the family narrative substance and beauty. She is still remembered as the "Pusher," for she realized before it was proven that lifetime income and well-being were directly related to the level of one's educational achievement. Two of the five children were valedictorians of their high school class, primarily, I suspect not because they were smarter but because she urged, encouraged, pushed, and rewarded school success. All five children did some college study, four of the five received college degrees, two of the five earned advanced degrees, one was named "teacher of the year," and another earned an outstanding teaching award and a distinguished alumnus award. Though she was heartbroken that with an A in organic chemistry, I did not choose to go into medicine, she could transcend that moment of personal disappointment to write in her last letter before her death, "I am so proud of you." Received when I was in a frenzy, preparing for my doctoral examination, the letter sadly slipped from my grasp.

There are stories we hear, the stories we tell, and the stories we inhabit that define who we are and serve as memory keepers. One such story of my childhood deals with the way shed tears reveal core values. I can still remember the first time I saw my tough mother cry. As a curious five-year-old in 1936, I came into our large farmhouse kitchen to find her in a serious argument with my Dad. They should have been happy, for just the night before, my oldest brother, Franklin, had graduated from high school as the valedictorian of his class and delivered a nice little talk scripted by the principal. As I stood on the edge of the room, eavesdropping, I heard my Dad say, "I just don't know how we can do it [i.e., send him to a technical college]. The drought is really bad [the 1936 rainfall totals in Arkansas fell fifteen inches short of normal.] We are just scraping by; we have four other kids to think about. We could lose everything." Her body shook with sobs as she muttered through her tears, "Where there is a will, there is a way." The next thing I remember from that exchange was my mother packing a bag lunch for Franklin for his bus trip to the technical college. How she won that argument or how they were able to support that venture, I do not know. The Arkansas family income *per year* in 1936 at $250 was barely half the national average. Maybe Grandma pitched in to help her little "Liebling." When he graduated from high school, she did give him one of her precious hoarded fifty-dollar gold pieces, a coin that his daughters still have. Or perhaps part of the $600 government bonus for Dad's military service in WWI supported this venture. I simply do not know.

I do know that that moment in the family story was pivotal, for even though Franklin's college was interrupted by the military draft early in 1940, it would be resumed after WWII. He would go on to complete his master's degree in history on the GI Bill and would become the school principal in nearby Bald Knob. He would preside over the integration of the school that happened without incident and would someday be the caregiver for both parents and our beloved Uncle Leo. Had not the Pusher won that argument, life could have been very different for the rest of us.

Ever after Daddy honored that service, and though he was basically a kindly soul, he made no attempt to conceal his contempt for draft dodgers. When I entered the service as an Air Force chaplain, the circle was complete. Every male of my family, descended from a once-scorned German immigrant couple, risked everything for this country, and all miraculously survived. But Sister Wanda suffered the greatest loss when chief warrant officer husband, Wayne, died of cancer induced by Agent Orange exposure from multiple Vietnam tours of duty as a helicopter pilot.

3. Neighborhood Stories

The annual spring-cleaning of the Smith (Schmidt) cemetery provided the setting for sharing a rich repository of stories. Though founded on the farmland mentioned in episode one, the cemetery became a neighborhood grave site. Established in the late nineteenth century, it would then cost nothing to claim a grave site there and still does not. And the result of this openness contributed mightily to the richness and variety of the stories exchanged at a burial or a spring-cleaning.

This cemetery ritual encouraged the recitation of the grand story the community inhabited; it gave the community strength to endure life's harsh demands and tragic surprises; it offered a bridge across the fuzzy line between the living and the dead; it became a vehicle of giving thanks for the sacrifices made on its behalf; it provided an occasion for entertainment, laughter, and the celebration of the ties that bind those in the present, and most importantly, it reminded the community of the lessons learned from its story that they were prone to forget. Through this muscular ritual, the persons who lived, suffered, and died did not just live once upon a time but were experienced in this ritualistic act as contemporaries still influencing this world. Some writers these days wonder if such living history is worth remembering. Their sentiments, some think, were well articulated by an English philosopher over a century ago.

"We must give it up, the speechless past . . . Lost is lost, gone is gone, forever," said Palgrave in 1865 in London. My childhood memory of those springtime events was resurrected by my participation in this annual event in March 1999 and still speaks a contrary message. As in days past, we gathered there early in the spring before the snakes came out to clean the country cemetery two miles east of Russell, Arkansas. This ritual spurred the memory of vital ties to ancestors and their narratives. It recited stories that still inspire, remind, and instruct. Ninety-year-old Vennie (i.e., Elvina) Kohl set out to cover the two miles by foot to clean the graves of her immigrant parents and five siblings who died as infants. Someone had curiously chiseled the date of her father's death off of the grave marker. Since she was born not nine months but a year after his death, a previous generation would have ridiculed her claim to legitimacy; that emblem of shame simply had to go. *Good work*, I thought, *whoever did it.*

Though weakened by a stroke, the son of Uncle Jake senior, cousin Jakie Roetzel, now eighty-nine, had insisted on coming to this event in spite of the strenuous objections of his daughter. Nancy was afraid he would be so caught up in the moment that he would overexert and die of a stroke. But in spite of her strenuous efforts to dissuade him, he was adamant.

"I'm goin'," he muttered, and he was there sharing the moment. Throughout the morning, our ranks swelled and swarmed over the gentle knoll overlooking the creek bottom to reclaim the space invaded by weeds, snakes, brush, and poison ivy.

The buzz of saws, the swish of rakes, the snip of clippers, the crackling fire, and the *chop-chop* of hoes mingled with bursts of laughter. Melanie hugged cousins she had not seen in ten years, and cousin Juanita reminisced with childhood friends from high school days. I huddled with a few teenagers to translate a German inscription on their great-great-grandmother's tombstone and to decipher a Goethe poem on the grave marker of her brother, Richard, whom influenza claimed just two decades after their emigration from Germany.

During the pauses, we gathered around Jakie, huddled in the shade of the fire-scarred oak that stood sentinel over this sacred space night and day, winter and summer, for over a century. A lifetime in the field had hardened his features, roughened the backs of his hands, and imbued his speech with a simple, beautiful directness. Though feeble, he presided over a litany of remembrance that raised the dead from their tombs and graced our ritualistic act. With a plot plan in his head, he moved from grave to grave with stories of love and hate, sex and violence, stark tragedy and generosity.

He pointed to the unmarked grave in the corner by the road that still holds the remains of the six men who died in the sawmill explosion nearby. "It was a cold, frosty morning," he noted, "when someone opened the valve, letting ice-cold water into a red-hot boiler. The blast was horrific. Uncle Henry, who was standing on a log nearby, cheated death when a piece of the exploding boiler narrowly missed his head. I was just four or five at the time. I remember the women rushing to the mill and crying and Mamma trying to help, but there was little she could do but hug the survivors and weep with them."

Pointing to other graves, he then told how Jim Bottomy shot Dave Bennings in a jealous rage and how Pete Weber, who could not swim, drowned trying to move livestock from the flooded bottoms to higher ground. He laced these tragic stories with tales full of poignancy. Pointing to a grave at our feet, "That is Grace Schnebly's sister, who died at twenty-two. She was pregnant with their second child, but she lost the baby and died of complications. Having no money for a tombstone, her husband poured concrete over her grave and, with a nail, scratched into the wet cement 'Agnes Barnett, 1910–1932.' He left a hole for flowers in the middle. Soon after he set out with his son for California and never came back. So Agnes lies there alone." I noticed, however, that she is not entirely alone, for there were fresh jonquils on her grave.

By the old sentinel oak, we paused by a small circle of stones with no marker. Jakie began, "That is the grave of a baby of a really, really, really poor couple. The pregnancy went badly, but they could not afford a doctor. When the time came, the midwife did what she could, but it was not enough. The baby died. The couple was so poor, they could not afford a casket, not even a cheap pine box, and they would not bury the child in a cardboard box in the backyard. Their neighbor, brother Otto, was the best carpenter around; he built his house with his own hands, and it was really somethin'; [he pointed] it still stands there on the corner. And Nellie, his wife, was a wonderful seamstress. Well, Otto made a small casket from cherrywood he had; it was real purty. Nellie made clothes for the little girl, dressed her and laid her on a cushion in the beautiful cherry coffin. Otto and the husband dug the grave, and Nellie joined them as they gently placed the baby there." I could not help but note that heaven must still be smiling on that kind deed, for a small cluster of violets had sprung up voluntarily on the grave to offer nature's blessing.

When we paused for a picnic, Jakie, who had hobbled into the cemetery in the early morning, seemed stronger. It was as if he was drawing energy from the stories he told, from the dead whom he resurrected with stories to share this moment, and from their examples that still offer an antidote to dark impulses. We all were energized by those plunges into the past.

At the end of the day, as our caravan snaked its way through the wheat field to the main road, I was a bit wiser. I better understood why 5,000 years ago, the Sumerians called the Amorites subhuman because they did not bury their dead. I better understood why 3,000 years ago, the Phoenicians saved the ashes and bones from their cremations in their most elegant pottery. I better understood why 2,500 years ago, the Greeks and Jews called the refusal of burial a barbaric act and the denial of a funeral the cruelest of punishments. I better understood why American Indians believe cemeteries are sacred, and I better understood why early Christians bought burial sites for the poor to save their bodies from being discarded on the Corinthian garbage dump. The importance of burial was hardly just because it was so offensive to deny the dead a place of rest. It was criminal because it robbed them of a voice; at least for the ancients, a person who died did not cease being a person and still had influence. As long as there are storytellers like Jakie and people who visit or clean the cemeteries, contrary to what Palgrave said, the past will not be "a speechless past." On our day of cemetery cleaning, we learned that a graveyard can be more than a sanctuary of grief, more than a place where we mingle the salt of our sweat with the salt of tears spilled in grief, and more than a plaque-dotted park that we pay others to keep. The cemetery is a great place to tell stories, to have picnics, and to recognize our debt and connection with those remembered who still inhabit our dreams.

Unfortunately, now, with the decline of that communal sense, the Smith cemetery has fallen into disrepair; it is overgrown with brush and weeds and mean spirits who no longer revere, learn from, or inhabit that narrative have vandalized scores of headstones, leaving them in shambles. The desecration is so painful that I feel I must recite the stories to transport the reader to a more humane, ennobling, and haunting possibility and to give voice to the dead who are people also. The experiences recalled here, like those with ties to thousands of small, untended, ill-kept burial spots in our country, remain to challenge the dark impulses of perfidy and to discredit the bootstrap philosophy of rugged American individualism. Cemeteries are memory keepers, and we are made the poorer without them. The stories told there do more than link the present with the past; they offer also a glimpse of future possibility. These accounts lead me to state that a people without stories is a people without compassion or imagination. Stories are the most important feature of resistance to bigoted, selfish, mean-spirited, subhuman, intellectual bankruptcy. Earlier I noted that those who have no past have no present, and now I would add no future as well.

It is worth noting that all other great world religions of the present and many of the distant past used stories to speak of their origins and destiny. Being ignorant of history, of a people's story, is the most toxic and even fatal form of amnesia. Stories provide a living window onto how peoples express their innermost imaginings and hopes and impose order on even a tortured human experience. In every story, there are dark chapters that also need remembering lest we attempt to make the past a fantasy without ugly human impulses.

This storied experience of the past was meant to deal with what was true in the deepest sense and honest about the propensity to perpetuate evil. The story I recall that most shaped me was peopled by the persons and forces above, but there were times in the emergence of that story that we could remember but refused to endorse or that were overridden by humane and even glorious gestures. For example, we knew of the time a robber broke into Grandma's unlocked house, stole all of her stash of money from her cotton crop, and then burned the house to the ground to hide the evidence. Neighbors simply would not let that gesture go unanswered. They all gathered at the homeplace and set about rebuilding a house for her that was more beautiful and serviceable than the old one. There was also the time when a neighbor sought to hire a friend to assassinate Grandma to lay claim to her property. In spite of those dark chapters, every gesture of the storytelling exercise kindled hope.

Chapter 3

Work, Sweat, and Tears

THE SINE QUA non for survival on an Arkansas farm during the Great Depression was work, very sweaty hard work. A small debt, a careless moment, an overdue loan, or a killer drought brought countless families face-to-face with bankruptcy. Hard realities, accidents, crippling illness, or sudden death could also steal a livelihood. Just so, a train accident and a rattlesnake bite snuffed out the lives of my parents' dads and left young widows to sink or swim. Debt-free land, family support, good health, and grit helped Grandma Roetzel through the Great Depression. Her four kids left school to help, and together they kept the ship afloat. Mom's mom, Grandma Pettit, was less fortunate. After her Irish immigrant blacksmith husband stepped in front of a train, he left no land, no money, and three kids to feed and clothe.

Why he was hit is a great mystery. Did he commit suicide to escape penury? Even Mom wondered. Rushing for home, did he make a fatal mistake? Some thought that was likely also. No one knew. The family's recent medical history points to a bout of hypoglycemia, or a low–blood sugar attack, that addled him. Great-granddaughter Lisa and I both inherited our hypoglycemia, and while neither is diabetic, we both experience low–blood sugar episodes. Fortunately, with excellent medical care, we can cope and live active, productive lives. My experience suggests that at the end of a hard day, when Grampa Pettit's blood sugar was very low, he might have stepped in front of a train without ever hearing or seeing the steam locomotive bearing down on him.

Whatever the cause, he left behind a young widow with no income, no prospects of a job, three children, and not enough cash from her insurance settlement to keep the children. With widespread prejudice against Irish immigrants, no one rushed to assist her. It was two older brothers who rescued her from her desperate plight. One took the boy, and another raised Mom and sister Ora to save them from the state run orphanage. That help made it possible for Grandma Pettit to sustain herself with the small monthly check from the railroad insurance payment.

1. Wonder Woman at Work

The brother raising Mama and Ora farmed a plot adjoining the Roetzel place, allowing Mom and Dad to grow up as neighbors. After third grade, like many farm kids elsewhere, they left school to work in home and field. That bitter shared experience steeled the resolve of our parents to provide for their children the education denied them. Growing up next door, Mom and Dad fell in love, married, and turned to the one thing they knew—tilling the soil (see 1918 appendix photo of young couple). With determination, hard work, and family support, they outlasted the Great Depression and raised five children. I came into the family late (1931) and had a ringside seat to view and share in their struggles.

Early to bed and early to rise meant being up at four thirty for the day ahead. Mom was up shuffling about in her pale, old, loose-fitting, homemade housedress, preparing a hearty breakfast to launch our day. The memory of those luscious breakfast smells wafting through the house still makes my mouth water. There was the odor of hot biscuits to be mixed with steamy gravy; there was the scent of sizzling slab bacon mingling with the fragrance of sorghum molasses on freshly buttered biscuits. There was the subtle aroma of hot oatmeal and that of leftover warmed-up peach cobbler; those smells excited our taste buds, and the meal fueled our bodies for the day ahead. Some estimate each member of a Depression farm family consumed about five thousand calories a day; if so, all of it was needed to service the day's tasks. None of us was obese.

Against the curse that Genesis 3:10 laid on Adam, "In the sweat of your face you shall eat bread" (RSV), never did Mom think of hard work as a curse—necessary, yes, but a curse for wrongs committed, no. There was a certain dignity to the work she and we kids did, but she rejected as a total lie the view that suffering, pain, and onerous hard work was imposed on us by God to make us stronger. For us that work requirement was obligatory and imposed limits to one's full development. Its everyday claims meant there were no summer church-camp experience, no Bible school interludes, no music lessons, no time for drawing and painting, and no leisure for summer classes or reading. We all, adults *and* children, simply took for granted that work was *the* necessary life condition. Sickness could allow temporary exemptions, but they were thankfully rare.

Attending church revivals or tent meetings was a summer ritual and a diversion that offered social engagement and religious exposure. We liked seeing friends and neighbors and enjoyed listening to imported gospel singing talent, but both parents dismissed the evangelical calls to "repent and be born agin'" as attempts to bag conversion trophies. Dad's aside to me after an aggressive attempt to "save" him was caustic: "I am more interested in what a person does than in what he says about bein' saved." He saw too many "born agins" more interested in posturing than serving. Those simple parents were certainly "spiritual" or religious but not sympathetic to fundamentalist Christianity.

Mom was more critical than Dad. She bristled at the claim that the Depression's hard times were God's punishment for sin and were meant to discourage dependence on FDR's social programs. She had read the same texts the preachers quoted, and she knew Isaiah's punishment formula: "**Speak tenderly** to Jerusalem and cry to her that her warfare is ended, that her iniquity is pardoned, that she has received from the Lord's hand double for all her sin" (40:2, my emphasis). Isaiah's account of God's math of "double" punishment for sin was too harsh, she muttered, but the focus on pardon and tenderness was wonderful. She heatedly objected to the suggestion that

God caused the death of her father because of his or someone else's sin or that drought and floods were a form of divine punishment. The suggestion that the death of a neighbor's young son, Junior, was God's will disgusted her. "It was not God who kilt him," she fumed, "his appendix busted; he needed a doctor." Moreover, she quoted Jesus's words on doing God's will with alacrity: "Whoever, DOES the will of God is my brother, and sister, and mother" (Mark 3:35, RSV). She resented all religious boasting set off by a literalist reading of the Bible. And finally, after hearing a conservative Christian evangelist defend such a reading, she mused, "I wonder how he deals with the reference in the Psalms that the mountains 'clap their hands.'"

Even with her paltry third-grade education, her simple words expressed spiritual wisdom in a quiet, unpretentious, understated, almost apologetic way. As a child, I hardly saw it as wisdom, but in my later years, I have come to value it more. It came, I now think, from an honest soul who had suffered life's hard knocks and who searched for meaning in a biblical narrative, dealing with human struggles and a strategy to cope. Her wisdom spoken through the limits imposed by her third-grade education now reminds me of the wisdom captured by the ancient Greek Aeschylus in 1180 BCE: "There is advantage in the wisdom won from pain."*

When traveling evangelists criticized Roosevelt's New Deal programs for interfering in charity work that God wanted the church to do, she rather cynically observed that there was more than enough need to go around and to keep God, the New Deal, and the church quite busy.

Mom's focus was less on her sin than on the tasks at hand. Before the breakfast cleanup was done, she was already planning the early noonday meal, "dinner." Like breakfast, it too was heavy with calories. The meal usually opened with a slab of hickory-smoked ham, mashed potatoes and gravy, and beans—white, green, or lima—from the garden; then she served a thick slice of freshly baked white bread

---

* Aeschylus, "Eumenides," 1180 BCE, from *Latham's Quarterly*, "Fear," vol. x, number 3 (2017), p. 29.

for use to wipe plates clean, and the meal was topped off with a slice of apple pie or a serving of hot berry cobbler and rich Jersey cream.

During White River overflows, trotlines in the backwaters snared catfish for a special treat and a welcome relief from the daily pork offerings. Trotlines were long lines with short drops evenly spaced with hooks and bait and could be left untended for hours and later "run" to remove the catch. Trotlines were the instrument of choice for catching catfish in the river and in the overflowing "backwaters" in the bottoms. When the catch was delivered, Mom rolled the pieces in meal and fried them in lard to a crusty brown. Her catfish with fried okra and potatoes or hush puppies usually prompted "Yums" that lit her stolid countenance with a puckish smile. She knew she was good at what she did, and she took pleasure in being recognized as the master of her domain.

Normal dinner leftovers most often formed the basis of the evening "supper" meal. They were often spruced up with cracklin' (not crackling) bread and "killed" leaf lettuce wilted with a dash of hot bacon grease and a touch of vinegar. Fried potato cakes, tomato and bread casserole, and breaded fried eggplant offered variety, and the leftover pie capped off the meal. However difficult survival was in the Great Depression, the farm families, unlike many urban poor, usually ate well. They did suffer, however, in other ways. There was little or no medical care available. One only visited a doctor or dentist with an emergency and never, ever for a regular checkup. Life expectancy was compromised. Subpar educational opportunities were the norm, and there was a dearth of modern amenities. There were few local regular-paying jobs on the railroad and in the mail service and school teaching, but they were available to only the better educated. Government programs like the WPA and CCC offered limited financial support, but those programs were almost totally staffed by white males and ended with the onset of the World War II.

As the family's sharpshooter and avid hunter and fisherman, Leonard did more than any other to bring variety to our table in winter. That fare included duck killed on the overflowing White River, quail, squirrel, rabbit from the farm fields and woods, and even an occasional opossum taken from one of his traps. As the most avid fisherman in the family, his hunting and fishing skills brought variety to the winter's menu. Pecan or karo-nut pies out of Mom's oven gave winter's table a special delicacy. Leonard and Mom both enjoyed their collaborative relationship, and he traded it for an MO (army lingo from *modus operandi* for *specialty*) as a cook for his US Marine company in WWII. To the variety he brought to our table, Mom concocted others from her store of canned vegetables put up for winter.

To offer up the soil's bounty on a daily basis, winter and summer, required constant, backbreaking toil. After supper, she took her place at the end of the living room couch to dip into her dog-eared King James Bible, but that respite was brief. While cooking was the most important part of Mom's priesthood, it was only a fraction of her daily chores. She had a large garden to plant and tend; from it came onions, spinach, radishes, cucumbers, lettuce, squash, beets, garlic, eggplant, cabbage, Irish and sweet potatoes, beans, black-eyed peas, leeks, bell peppers, carrots, and small hot red peppers, sage, early and late tomatoes, cantaloupe, watermelon, turnips, pumpkins, and grapes. From it also she prepared sauerkraut, pickles, chowchow, and pepper salts. The garlic, onions, sage, and hot red peppers she hung on the wall, waiting to be used to flavor the liverwurst at "hog killing" time.

On Mondays she did the family wash in a number three tub on the back porch. Using her homemade lye soap to scrub clothes clean on a metal rubboard, she wrung them by hand and hung them out to dry on the backyard clothesline. When they were dry, she brought them in and mended and pressed them with flat irons heated on her Home Comfort wood-fired stove. From the empty fifty-pound flour sacks, she sewed dresses for sister Wanda. In the winter months, she pieced together quilt covers from random scraps of cloth she had saved and hung the quilt on a frame suspended from the kitchen ceiling over the "dinner table" that she could lower in spare moments to sew our quilts for winter. Those covers, the yard plantings, and food creations and presentations were her offerings of a kind of rustic art.

In addition to those multiple tasks in and around the house, she milked cows, skimmed and sold the cream, managed the strawberry-harvest packing shed, and raised a hundred chickens in her large kitchen and gradually moved them to their own yard. When they matured and gained access to nests in the chicken house, she gathered their eggs and washed and crated them for use as barter for flour, salt, sugar, coffee, and oatmeal. Occasionally she traded any surplus for a nice chunk of cheese from Ward's store in Bradford.

Once she teamed with Dad to shell pecans for sale and purchased our first battery-powered radio with an outdoor antenna and a short-wave reception when the automobile battery was fully charged. Curious neighbors often gathered in our living room to listen to this novelty and to enjoy Westerns, the Grand Ole Opry, radio evangelists, newscasts, country Western music, Roosevelt's fireside chats, *and Lum and Abner*. At critical moments of listening, my Dad would pay Wanda and me a penny a minute to sit quietly as they listened to programs without interruption.

The Sunday dinners Mom prepared were always special. We were almost always joined by bachelor Uncle Leo, Dad's soul mate and our substitute Grandpa, sometimes the minister, and often a relative or school friend. With no recess from her work to rest or play, she simply had to ignore the commandment to do no work on the Sabbath. On those days, she often created special treats like a multi-layered coconut or chocolate cake that was attractive *and* delicious.

The formula for her cooking exercises was locked in her head. There was no cookbook in her kitchen. The recipes for her dishes were stored in her memory, and in preparing them, she doctored them to taste. This mode of being and operation, I suspect, was in no way unusual. Books were expensive, and kitchen shelf space and budgets were limited. So "making do" was the modus operandi for most poor farm women of the Great Depression. Small wonder that many died young. Interestingly, a recent large Oxford University Press volume on food offers no accounting of the special farm food rituals we knew.

Like most farm parents wearied by the heavy workload and length of workdays, she hoped her children would have a more humane and financially rewarding future. Mom well knew that academic achievement would likely open doors to a richer, fuller, and more promising life. That knowledge earned her the title of Pusher. On the big issues, however, a sober realism tempered her hopes for our future. She was aware of the possibilities hidden in our young breasts, but she also well knew the odds against their full realization. Many neighbors also worked hard but gained few rewards. She well knew there was no transcendent accounting law in the sky that guaranteed reward for hard work. One had to be realistic and a bit lucky. That realism, I suspect, protected her from cynicism when plans went awry. Nevertheless, her combination of idealism and realism was a recipe for change.

Her constant entrepreneurial skills contributed mightily to our survival. With the spare cash she earned, she purchased incidentals—linoleum rugs for the bare wooden floors, oilcloth for the table, a sewing machine, materials for a new school dress for Wanda, and kitchenware. Without her efforts, diligence, and imagination, we could not have kept our farm during the Great Depression when so many neighbors lost theirs. She gave her best and expected that of all of us. It is impossible to overestimate the importance of the load she carried or the role she played in urging all of us to prepare ourselves for a more fulfilling life. I still find it rather amazing that all of us children had some academic experience beyond high school, and all had fulfilling careers. Many factors contributed to that success and service, but the greatest of all was that the Pusher provided.

2. Child Labor

While studies of the Great Depression regularly note the oppressive workload farm life imposed on women *and* men, few note the burden shared by children. The child labor laws came for a more industrial setting, and thankfully, they protected young children from crass exploitation in sweatshop factories, and today's "prophets" rightly warn against the purchase of products produced in foreign countries by child labor. As victims of greed and exploitation, children around the world suffer mightily, and praise is due to those who shine a light on such mean-spirited grubbing for money. From earliest childhood, however, Wanda and I, like children of other farm families, shared in the farm's workload. For years we always worked as a team. At just three or four, we churned cream for butter, taking turns at the dasher. We stacked the cook- and heating-stove kindling and wood that was cut, split, and piled in the backyard. In our wagon, we hauled and piled that wood onto the appropriate porches—small cookstove wood on the back porch, heating stove wood on the front. We washed and dried dishes as a pair; we peeled potatoes, and we took turns pumping water for the animals. With our small hands, we could reach through the mouths of canning jars to wash and rinse them for later use, and our small hands could also fit inside kerosene lamp globes to clean them. During the hot summer months, we carried fresh, cool well water to field workers. (*A sad note*: The clean, cool water from almost all of those wonderful farm wells is now polluted by fracking and pesticides and is unfit for human *or* animal consumption.) Together, we chopped (i.e., weeded and thinned) cotton, hoed strawberries, tended the garden, and walked a quarter mile to our mailbox to fetch the daily delivery and Sunday's *Arkansas Gazette*. We paired to weed, fertilize, and pick strawberries, and during the late-summer school vacation, we picked cotton side by side. We planted cut potatoes and later assisted with the harvest, "the pickup." We hired ourselves out at fifty cents a day to chop cotton for Uncle and, with that money, bought our own clothes and shoes for school. In late spring and early summer, we picked wild blackberries for cobblers and canning. For the great hog-killin' event in midwinter, we were allowed to play hooky from school to help with the butchering. We poured hot water into the intestines of the pigs to clean them for the link sausage (small intestine) or liverwurst (large intestine). We took turns at the crank of the sausage grinder to make the fillings. On occasion we fed onions, sage, and pepper into the mix to season the wurst.

Some families hired a travelling butcher team to do this unseemly chore, but our hog killin' was a local and social occasion. It brought uncles, aunt, brothers, and cousins all together to share in the festival. The air was full of conversations and peals of laughter. Before daybreak Daddy started the fires under the large black cast-iron kettles. Uncle was busy sharpening the butchering knives to a razor's edge and then serving as the one who bled the animals after the slaughter, supervised the cleaning, and carved the slaughter. The women supervised the sausage making, the rendering of lard, and meal preparations. When the long day finally ended at dusk, each bone-tired family left with two or three significant pieces of fresh meat and wurst. Later it would be Dad who would cook the salt brine to cure the pork in fifty-gallon wooden barrels and then remove and hang it to be smoked in the specially prepared house.

After this daylong recess, Wanda and I returned to our one-room country school. It was a simple building without electricity, running water, or central heat. A large heating stove stood at the center of the room to make the temperature bearable but not necessarily comfortable. But true to its name, the White School (taking its name from the White River) was one of the few in the neighborhood painted white. An outdoor hand pump provided our washing and drinking needs, special gender-specific privies constructed by the WPA stood at opposite ends of the school yard, and that yard had no play equipment but did offer room for games and space for eating our bag lunches.

After walking the one and a half miles to school, Wanda and I took our separate places among forty other pupils. The school day opened with the Pledge of Allegiance then a story told or read by the teacher and ended with a song. The teacher chose different students to lead the singing; even I had a turn. Sometimes we sang "My Country, 'Tis of Thee," folk, popular, and even some gospel songs. After this opening ritual, the real schoolwork began in the basics: arithmetic, reading, spelling, writing, geography, history, and civics. With forty pupils and eight grades sharing one room, it was simply impossible for any teacher to supervise every pupil in every subject. They simply had to call on students with special strengths to assist. With my strength in math, I was pushed through four grades in two years, and at eight or nine, I had my first taste of teaching—a task I liked and was able to do with joy until the end of my career. Wanda helped with reading, spelling, and writing, and those experiences influenced our decisions to become teachers.

Recess offered ways to release pent-up energy in games like "Red Rover, Red Rover, Red Rover, come over," softball, and tag. Friday ended with a math (cipher match) and/or a spelling contest. During the normal day, there was time for reading out loud and for doing homework. The school library was tiny, but its collection held important works by Mark Twain, Dickens, Lewis Carrol, and Jonathan Swift and copies of *Grimms' Fairy Tales*. Although there were no plantations in the area, there was a significant African American community in a town five miles away that was segregated by the railroad. I do not recall a legacy of racial hatred expressed in the home, but I do remember being puzzled that in the Bald Knob Railroad Depot, there were separate restrooms and fountains for "colored." At almost every level, racial division and prejudice was institutionalized. The very fact that schools were not integrated and the blacks who lived on one side of the street in shanties only crossed that boundary to work as maids, cooks, janitors or construction workers and then had to return to their segregated space at night reinforced discriminatory habits. My awareness of the unfairness of this system began early. I remember reading Mark Twain's *Adventures of Huckleberry Finn*, which made me aware of how unfair segregation was. Kids have to be taught racism and sexism, and fortunately, I had been spared such indoctrination. In chapter 16 of Twain's book, I identified strongly with Huck, for whom his friendship with Jim was more important than the threat of hell for lying as he paddled Jim across the Mississippi into Illinois to liberate him from his bondage to Ms. Watson, his owner. I vividly recall Huck's dilemma; he was lectured to never tell a lie, and when he did so to save Jim from being detected, he felt so dirty and mean. If questioned on Jim's whereabouts, he faced a terrible dilemma; he would either have to lie or to betray his dearest friend. No matter what he did, his conscience would shame and scold. Facing this impossible dilemma, Huck says, "If I had a yaller dog and he had no more sense than my conscience, I'd poison him."

Twain's works and the example of a small socially aware church prepared Wanda and me in important ways for later involvement in the civil rights struggle.*

Sister Wanda and I stood by and defended each other in the hard times. Even though I was small, my farm work hardened me, and once I felt called on to stand up to the school bully who was picking on Wanda and her friend Rosemary Banks; that physical encounter put an end to his taunts and attempts to bully. And she also stood up for me when she saw me reduced to tears by older students poking fun at my sandwich of homemade bread and liverwurst. Their white "store-bought" Wonder Bread entitled them, they thought, to ridicule my humble lunch. Wanda must have well made her case to the teacher, for I can still see her coming out the school building, breathing fire. The names of those antagonists were forever etched in my memory, and their forced apologies did not entirely remove the hurt. My parents, who saw beauty as a character issue, encouraged me to feel sorry for the offenders so prone to such ugliness.

Wanda and I also shared a common life in the Methodist church, populated early on by many German Lutheran immigrants who turned Methodist because their circuit riders served pastoral needs left unmet by their Lutheran church. We joined the church at the same time, attended worship and summer "revivals" together, and sat in the same youth group and Sunday school class. With all of its faults, that church was unlike neighboring fundamentalist churches that focused on individual salvation to the virtual exclusion of any emphasis on social outreach to the needy, social justice, or historical critical study of the Bible. That little church took in young girls pregnant out of wedlock who felt publicly shamed and abandoned; it loved, supported, encouraged, and nurtured them toward meaningful, fulfilling lives. I can still name them all. Against the social prejudice against gays, that church's best Sunday school teacher was the gay superintendent from the local high school. And thankfully, that legacy has endured as that tiny church runs a vital after-school program for disadvantaged, needy, poor, and mixed-race kids from

---

* Mark Twain, *Adventures of Huckleberry Finn,* chapter 16.

a neighboring town and school. It is literally the salt of their earth, leavening the entire community.

From being coached by that socially active church, Wanda would one day be a teacher in the Charleston, Arkansas, elementary school, the first in the state to integrate without incident. (Note: I write this on the sixtieth anniversary of the integration of Central High School in Little Rock under the guard of a 101st Airborne unit.) She attended that church with a local attorney, Dale Bumpers, who would one day become Senator Bumpers, and they assisted with the merger of that church with a local black Methodist congregation.

My own experience was similar at Hendrix College, where along with a group of snotty young students and alums, we challenged the president and the trustees to institute open admission to the college. We did not win that battle, but in the end, our cause won out. When I entered the Air Force chaplaincy, I deliberately asked to be elected to the requisite elder's orders by the Methodist black Central Jurisdiction that had been segregated in the earlier church union as a concession to Southern segregationists. Later I had the high honor as a pastor to share the platform with Martin Luther King Jr. Our whole lives have been given to tasks that removed walls that divide, and the inspiration for that activity came from our family, our one-room school, and a small, struggling church.

3. Teamwork with Dad

World War II intervened to disrupt the farm teamwork that Wanda and I practiced in our early years. With the older brothers taken by the military, the need for me in the fields separated us. At that moment, we both went from being children to being adults and thus skipped adolescence. That direct move from childhood to adulthood, I now understand, was fairly common among farm children.

The war reassigned me to Dad's team. We linked arms to do the field preparation, the planting, tilling, and harvesting of crops. With him I learned to love the smell of freshly turned soil and spring's blossoms. We shared the excitement, promise, and mystery of the burst of new life in the spring and the satisfaction a good harvest brought. The optimism I came to have about life and the human prospect was cultivated in that relationship. From him I learned the importance of generosity and service. He served as a member of the school board, the church board, the church-building committee, and the local election commission, and when a neighbor came needing help, he freely offered it. With the only car in the neighborhood, he rushed a childhood friend to the doctor after he was severely burned in a grass fire. He loaned scarce dollars to a desperate cousin sharecropper, and he sent me to prepare a neighbor's garden for spring planting. He modeled my sense of the obligation to serve the needy and to respond to requests for help. From him I learned that one's greatest and most important investment is in human life.

With the brothers all in military service, I was assigned to the tasks they once performed. When just eleven, I was hand cranking the Model A John Deere tractor my dad and Uncle shared (see appendix picture). Hooked to breaking plow, disc, and harrow, I prepared the fields for planting and tilling. When allowed to purchase a smaller Model B John Deere (with a starter and lights!), my field duties expanded. Those tasks, I felt, dignified me as a "big boy," authorized me to drive the truck around the farm and on the backcountry roads, and entitled me to drive Uncle home after our shopping trips for groceries. His trust in my driving skill may have been reckless, but it built my confidence.

Although I had fed the mules and cows earlier when the brothers left for service, I quickly learned to harness, hitch, and drive the mule team and to treasure the special relationship of respect and even affection that developed. The animals seemed to realize an obligation to school this green, vulnerable, and ignorant kid and to care for his life.

Those shared tasks enriched my relationship with Daddy. We were work partners tending the farm and its tasks. In the winter, we cut wood together, and I took my place on the other end of the crosscut saw to cut wood for heating and cooking. We felled, split, and sharpened white oak logs for fence posts we used to mend fences. From him I learned the names of all of the trees in the forest, and I came to see that the naming was no control mechanism but an agency of recognition and acceptance. We gathered the corn with Uncle, and we worked with a mule team that knew and responded instantly to our verbal commands. We hauled loose hay together with Uncle on the wagon, arranging the load, and Daddy and I on the ground, pitching the hay onto the wagon hayrack. When we brought the loaded wagon to the barn, we set the two-pronged hayfork into the load and drove Bud and Tom to hoist the hay by rope and pulley into the barn loft. From Dad I learned to split and plane cypress shingles to patch the leaky house and barn roofs, and together we loaded and spread barn manure on the fields to fertilize the crops. From him I also learned the importance of attention to detail and of empathy for all living creatures. I sat by the hour, watching him craft a jon boat, and I was amazed at its launch that it did not leak. A jon boat was a stable flat-bottomed wooden boat that would ride over the waves rather than slice through them and was stable and ideal for fishing, paddling, and all water exercises. The relationship with Dad as we shared tasks infected me with the can-do spirit that the Depression demanded for survival and that remained later to serve me as a university-committee member and departmental chair.

I embraced his sense of kinship with other living creatures. That sense later enabled me to capture a swarm of honeybees without sting or fear. Since my Dad was allergic to beestings, I volunteered to scrape the bees into a wooden hive, in which they were to live and work, and later without mask or smoker, I "robbed" the hive of some of its honey while leaving enough for the hive for winter. The taste of that freshly stored and processed honey spread onto Mom's hot biscuits was indescribably delicious.

In the relationships farm life fostered, I felt loved, secure, and never hungry, but could I then say, as many now say of life in the Great Depression, "We didn't know we wuz poor"? The short answer to that question is an emphatic "No!" Even with all of the benefits offered in my family experience, I, nevertheless, knew we wuz poor! As I insist here, a child's view may not align with conventional adult wisdom or practice, but the view from below that children offer can provide insight into the human experience.

4. I Knew We Wuz Poor

It is true we had delicious and abundant food; we had a good place to sleep, and we had opportunities to play, but still, there were times as a child when I was acutely conscious of our poverty. When we went to town, I saw that people there lived in painted houses, and our board-and-batten house was unpainted. In town I noticed that the boys my age wore pants, and none wore hand-me-down patched Tuf Nut overalls. I noticed that they wore nice shoes year-round while, except for school days, I went barefoot from April to September. They had electricity; we had none. They read by bright lamps, and I read by the pale light of a kerosene lamp. They had indoor plumbing and telephones while I took my bath in a number three washtub and drew our water for drinking, cooking, washing, and scrubbing. I easily saw that they were privileged in ways I was not. Until I graduated from high school, I had never spoken on a phone, never had a train ride, and only once crossed the state line. I could easily see that store owners and clerks wore suits, and my dad wore overalls. Even when paired with a clean blue denim work shirt, the clothes we wore signaled a lower status; I knew we wuz poor. Only at his mother's funeral and our wedding do I ever recall seeing my Dad in a suit and tie. Never do I recall seeing a young girl in town wearing a dress made from flower sacks as did Wanda until she was school-age.

My mother was so aware of her lower status that she always had me write her letters, even to my brothers in service. She could write, but she knew her grammar was faulty and her writing style crude. I could write standard English. We knew; we all knew, and as the little one, I especially knew, we wuz poor. On our trip to Ward's store in Bradford, I would notice that some farmers painted their barns red. I asked my dad if we could do that, but he shifted the conversation; he knew what I meant. Now I realize he could have said that the wide, long, weathered white oak planks siding our barn were more beauti-ful than any painted-red board imaginable, and he would have been right; maybe he also knew what I meant at a deeper level. The cracks between the barn's weathered planks were turned silky smooth by the licking tongues of cows reaching for an extra bite of hay; those cracks smoothed by animal tongues made their own point. Red paint would have hidden the poignancy and character of their intrusion.

One occasion I recall vividly illustrates my point. When brother Franklin was in the Army Air Corps, training with the troop carriers for D-Day on a base near Amarillo, Texas, he met and fell in love with a beautiful young woman whose name and address I still recall. She struck up a correspondence with the family, and all of my Mom's replies I crafted, and then I forged her signature. That charming young woman sent her picture, which stood on the dresser in the living room alongside that of handsome brother Sergeant Franklin in his freshly pressed army uniform; they remained there side by side until well after the war's end. In 1943 this young woman sent my mother a big bouquet on Mother's Day with the note "Love and best wishes on your day." Even though we children did pick wildflowers for untidy bouquets for Mom, I am certain that bouquet was the only bouquet my mother ever received from a florist.

Soon this young woman wrote, asking if she might visit us. Then came my moment of truth. Unlike my friends' houses in town, our farmhouse was made of unpainted oak board-and-batten construction. I was ashamed of the lack of amenities that townspeople took for granted. Cheap, crude linoleum, not woven rugs, covered our floors. The privy was over fifty yards from our house on the other side of the garden, and an old Sears catalogue provided the toilet paper. Not until 1948 did Roosevelt's Rural Electrification Program of 1933 reach us. We had no telephone. Mom suggested I write that beautiful young woman a letter with a word of welcome and to note that we were simple people without the advantages she might take for granted, *but* we would gladly welcome her. I was also to note that we had one thing in common—namely our love for Franklin. But I was so ashamed, I could not write the letter; I was certain that if she visited us, she would notice that we wuz poor. Mom could not write to explain my negligence, for then the young woman would know from her poor script and Arkansas slang that she had been deceived by my script. I still feel confident that she interpreted the absence of an invitation from us as a "No, you are not welcome." It was not that, however; it was rather "No, we are poor, dirty, shabbily dressed, and sometimes unbathed, stinky farm people; you would not like us."

Not long after my shameful negligence, Franklin was reassigned to duty in England, which was under heavy Luftwaffe bombardment. His air corps planes were special targets. The young and deeply loved woman gave up. She was afraid he would be killed and she would be left alone. Fearing he would never return, their long-distance relationship cooled. She met another, fell in love, and married him. I really loved that woman and felt enormous guilt over the breakup that my negligence may have caused. There were surely other factors, but I was unaware of them. I was just twelve at the time and did not understand that my mother was right; an honest, open letter might have been the most wonderful thing imaginable, and she might have visited and been absolutely inspired by the role food played in the warm hospitality we offered, the relationships we formed, the social distances it bridged, and the joyful life it affirmed. We will never know, but I do know now what drove my neglect and even malfeasance. I knew we wuz poor, and because of my insecurity, I felt inferior. I did not then know at twelve how to raise the question, "What is poverty, really?" Or "In other ways, are we not really rich?" "Who in the city, even Amarillo, has a mule like Bud for a friend?" She could have petted Bud with her own lily-white hand. But the sad story ended well. Technical Sergeant Franklin returned home after serving over six years in the army with a string of stripes on his arm and ribbons on the left side of his chest. After a time, he met and fell in love with another and married, and they had two beautiful and wonderful daughters whom my mother helped raise. Their presence is still a vivid expression of a story that ended well. But as a twelve-year-old, I could not see that far ahead, and I did not have the tools for dealing with the special mental challenges that the blood, sweat, and tears of farm life laid on us.

Though "we wuz poor," we were especially blessed, or rich, in the special sanctity given our work and the wonder excited by creatures of the world we inhabited, but I could not factor that into a letter even though, at a deep level, I knew it to be true. My simple poem below seeks to capture once more the premonitions of promise that I could not intuit as a child of the Great Depression.

Oh, Summer Night, you excited wonder in the
child I once was.
Your fireflies blinked in the darkness.
Your bats wiggled through the blackness.
Your owls hooted and prowled the forest.
Your gentle lightning unveiled the sky afar.
Your meteoroids streaked their fire earthward.
Oh, Night Sky, your memory still inspires
and humbles me.
I am so small!

Your dawn awakened day's creatures to their tasks.
Lazy monarchs arced from bloom to bloom.
Manic hummers dashed to sup nature's sweetness.
Nervous bees gathered nectar for winter's hive.
Shiny black snakes slithered into weeds, hiding.
Stolid terrapins hunkered down in roadside heat.
All creatures, great and small, at work.
You hallow all my toil.

Chapter 4

Surprises That Refreshed

WHILE BOREDOM AND isolation were hardly ills afflicting only farm families in the Great Depression, the trauma of the period aggravated those tendencies. Hunger, foreclosure, drought, bugs, illnesses, fire, dust storms, and tornados were real. Psychic ills, frustration, loneliness, weariness, and accidents also robbed families of peace. All threats combined made a toxic stew. Our isolation a quarter mile from the county road and the struggle to remain solvent and independent were wearing and constant. Those pressures, Mom thought, led her nephew farmer nearby to commit suicide. Farm families had no vacations to decompress and recharge. The only vacation my family ever had was a short road and camping trip into the Ozark hills in their first auto, a 1932 Model A Ford sedan. I was a year old, and Mom was pregnant with Wanda and miserable. She, nevertheless, so we were told, did the cooking and packing each morning for the next day's run through the Ozarks.

Facing a daily workload that allowed little time for socializing, tending flowers in the yard, or artistic outlets, Mom lobbied for a move to a building site on the farm we owned a half mile away at a lively county road intersection, a location that offered a stunning view of the nearby Ozark foothills. The sheer drudgery of her labor and its mindless, boring, repetitive nature fueled Mom's passion to move to escape bouts of depression. That move would have left behind barn, corncrib, chicken house, cotton shed, garden, smokehouse, and outdoor toilet. Field workers also and, yes, even children knew the weariness of farm work. The stupor induced by driving a tractor up and down a field for hours to break fresh earth for planting and to disc and harrow the soil was inescapable. I recall making speeches, giving lectures, offering legal defenses and preaching sermons to myself to break the monotony of driving the Model A Deere round and round. That experience helped me later understand why primitive Middle Eastern agrarian peoples invoked the law of the desert that obligated settlers to welcome strangers, wayfarers, or even enemies. It was more than kindness that informed that rule; it was the need for stimulation an outsider brought, even if that person were a stranger or alien.

Partly to address the burdens of rural farm life in the Great Depression, our home, like most, welcomed "peddlers," evangelists, salesmen of all types, and beggars. Hobos rarely came our way, for we were two miles from the train track, and it would hardly be worth a four mile walk for a crust of bread; but when they did come, my folks always offered food even when withholding cash. Mom and Dad even welcomed evangelical emissaries out to convert my dad. As a child, I sat quietly listening to the testimonials about how much the life of those "witnesses" reputedly improved after they were born agin', and I watched my dad as he quietly endured their pitch. When the pause came for a decision, he would thank them for coming and for their concern, shake their hand, and bid them goodbye. Their visits frightened me, for I did not want the product they were selling. I really loved my dad and did not want him to become like one of them. I never could understand exactly why Dad was on their hit list; maybe it was his kind, welcoming nature that made a visit low-risk. He would always patiently listen, but his independent nature and skepticism of overrighteousness made Ecclesiastes 7:16 one of his favorite Bible verses, "Be not righteous overmuch," a verse he also summoned to discourage boasting and bravado. True, I had an idealized view of my father. I saw him as a kind, generous, unselfish man whose piety moved him to care for anyone in need and to follow rather simple rules of language use that totally eschewed profanity and dishonesty. The hospitality my family offered, however, was no humanitarian gesture; visitors of whatever persuasion provided an interlude to a deadly, repetitive, boring daily regimen.

In the springtime, peddlers of patent medicines came calling. It was Mom who interacted with those brokers calling at mealtime to catch us during the break from fieldwork. She bought treatments for worms, antimalarial quinine, and bitter spring tonics that we children despised. The visits themselves, however, were a real tonic for the monotony fieldwork induced.

I vividly recall the visit of the stove salesman and his conversation with both Mom and Dad. He noted that Mom's old cookstove was worn out and a fire hazard. A fire on the farm would have been catastrophic, for there was no phone to summon help and no help to summon. A fire in one building that a grass fire kindled years after we left the place reduced all five to ashes. The salesman offered the perfect solution—a beautiful, safe white Home Comfort kitchen range with generous cooktop space, dampers that controlled the oven temperature and moderated the warming-oven temperature, and a large copper reservoir to heat bathwater. They bought the stove; it lasted for years and only gave way to a propane cookstove that I later purchased when I was a salaried Air Force chaplain. I made that purchase to spare my ailing dad his solitary woodcutting chores. Yet the gift was tainted by the memory of the altar-like presence the old Home Comfort range projected at the south end of the kitchen.

The visits of these sales*men* (always men) were a welcome antidote to the boredom, loneliness, and monotony of farm work. Rølvaag's *Giants in the Earth* makes the same point about the struggles of immigrant farm women to cope in South Dakota with the earth, winter, isolation, boredom, and prejudice that led to the "insane asylum." His poignant story recounted the wagon's springtime circuit to haul away delirious women after the snow melted. I knew of no woman in our circle who succumbed to mental illness, but I could understand the eagerness of my mom to relocate to a site that in the crassest practical terms made no sense. She wanted and needed more social interaction. And even though the old place would always be my real "home," my mom's mental health took priority.

Though all of those visits were memorable, it was another that still offers my most vivid recall. His visit came just weeks after a neighbor's teenage son died rather suddenly from a ruptured appendix with no medical attention. Almost as if scripted, an insurance salesman sat in our sitting room, making a pitch to Mom and Dad to purchase burial insurance for the kids. My parents well knew the tortured reality of infant and childhood mortality. Scores of young cousins once vital and active now lay in the Smith cemetery. There was little money available to buy burial insurance, but Dad and the salesman figured out a way. By extending the purchase period to twenty years with minimal payments each year, Dad agreed to buy a burial insurance policy for each of the five children that, upon maturity or death, would be worth $500. That sum seemed outlandish in the thirties, but the transaction I witnessed was no empty gesture. It was a caring response to the untimely, tragic, or accidental deaths of children and a loving gesture that protected no one but promised the unfortunate a dignified exit. Through good times and bad, Dad made those annual pension payments in August for twenty-five years. It was later, much later, as I set off with my family to graduate school, that Mom handed me the mature policy worth $500. Seeing firsthand the sacrifice, thoughtfulness, and love that informed more than twenty years of insurance payments, I just simply could not accept that money, but the policy was in my name, and I alone could submit it for redemption. So I immediately wrote Mom a check for $500 to cover the face value of the policy, and even that was a mere token of gratitude for the sacrifice made by both parents.

Another visit that was almost habitual was that of our surrogate grandpa, Uncle. His weekly Sunday supper visits were always welcomed. After Grandma died in the summer of '42, he lived alone and regularly shared a Sunday meal and company with us as long as I can remember. His visits were dominated mostly by small talk, speculation about the weather, and the crops, followed by a delicious meal. Before leaving he would slip small coins into the hands of Titter and me and join Dad to listen to Lum and Abner. As a part of the final stereotypical ritual, he would stand and say, "Well, I better be goin'." Dad's response was 100 percent predictable: "What's the hurry?" he would always mutter. Uncle, who was in no hurry, would stay for just a bit longer before he would stand, move toward the front door, and say, "I gotta go." Then there would be more exchanges about little or nothing before the final negotiation of parting. Finally, Dad would always say, "See ya later."

This ritual of parting, as predictable as was the ritual of the opening greeting, was supposed to ease or provide a smooth transition to the intruding absence. The advent of cell phones has sabotaged those old formulas of meeting and parting and the relationships that were cultivated by them, and that is a pity, for on the farm, those rituals helped us cope with some of the weariness that daily and unremitting toil laid on us. The reliability and structure of the rituals associated with Uncle's visit affirmed the depth, importance, and reliability of a human relationship that fostered a sense of deep security and trust in a shared hard life.

I can still remember the frenzy of activity a prospective visit by Grandma would trigger. The house had to be spotless, our beds had to be made, and our dirty clothes picked up and moved to a basket for washing; even windows were washed and wood stacked neatly. What drove this frenetic activity, I could hardly understand as a ten- to twelve-year-old, for Grandma was always full of hugs and kisses, but now I better understand my mother's frenzy; she did not want to be viewed as a bad mom, wife, or daughter-in-law. Being Irish she felt she had to work really hard to be accepted. But at a more fundamental level, there was the cultural norm. The advent of important or prestigious visitors required a welcome that would befit their status. Even those rare, stressful Grandma visits did more than affirm our family solidarity; they offered a moment of release from the everyday.

In addition to these predictable visits, there was the unexpected break that brought joy and lingering excitement. One such surprise ranks above all of the rest. Embedded in one of those joyful unexpected visits was a dark, painful tragedy. Its memory demanded that we think beyond our own hardships. It happened like this: Late one hot, sultry August afternoon in 1941, a strange automobile came roaring down our dirt road, trailed by a dust cloud; it skidded to a halt, and out of it stepped a smartly dressed trim young man in his summer naval whites. My mom recognized him immediately and screamed in euphoric delight, "Ross, Ross, Ross." This was her nephew, Chief Petty Officer Charles Ross Pettit, whose home base was far, far away in San Diego, California; he was home on leave. She had not seen him in years, but on a leave to visit his parents, Mom's brother, twenty-five miles to the north, he made time to visit Aunt Myrtle before shipping out. I was mesmerized by his august, tall, uniformed presence and the energy he exuded. I kept close by to eavesdrop and gawk.

When relatives came, the law of hospitality dictated that they stay for a meal. Immediately Mom set about preparing for this occasion with the one thing she knew, delicious food. I was in the chicken yard for the preparation launch. She walked into the yard in her sloppy, faded, long kitchen dress, pitched out a few grains of corn. The unsuspecting chickens raced to devour it; then suddenly her arm zipped out, snatched a rather plump young rooster by the leg, grasped his head, twirled his body, and once the head was separated, threw it to the ground as the beheaded body jumped about. I perfectly understood why the cluster of chickens fled in a panic. Then without hesitation, Mom began cleaning and preparing that sacrificial victim for a delicious fried-chicken dinner. My little brain felt the contrast—tragedy for the rooster and a succulent delight for us. My ten-year-old witness of this event has given me a lifelong appreciation for the stark brutality folded into the English metaphor to "wring the neck" of a foe. That cruel image still often haunts me when I eat the fried chicken, for which this unsuspecting victim was dedicated.

In the summer of 1941, when Ross came, Franklin had already been taken from our circle by the draft, and the two other brothers knew their turn would soon come. But we four gathered with our parents and Ross at the round oak table; I can still see those four heads, with Ross and Mom and Dad gathered around the table draped in a freshly wiped, brightly colored oilcloth. Wanda and I always shared the bench, but the adults had chairs. What a joyful and appropriate feast this was. Then too quickly darkness closed in, and Mom lit the coal oil lamps, signaling the end of the visit. Ross hugged us all, Mom cried, and Dad shook his hand and said, "Take care of yourself, Bub," which was no idle throwaway wish. It came from one who well knew the brutal nature of war from his combat experience in World War I. Knowing firsthand the horror of battle and seeing the grief it brought not just to other soldiers, buddies, and units but also to innocent women, children, and the elderly has understandably led thousands of voters to prefer a president with military experience, who has experienced the horror of war firsthand. Many feel such leaders are more likely to see war as a last resort in efforts to resolve international disputes. My feeble vocabulary seems so impoverished even now when it struggles to recount that story's ending.

We later had a brief note from Ross that came to our rural mailbox on route one about how much fun he had with us and how he hoped we could do it again "after this [i.e., the war] is over." He had earlier shared with us in confidence that he would be leaving from the San Diego naval station in a submarine, on which he would serve as chief petty officer. We now know that by December 7, 1941, he was at Pearl Harbor on the Arizona. His submarine was there for repairs. After the Japanese attack that Roosevelt called a day of "infamy," we waited for weeks and months, hoping against hope that there might someday be another visit from Ross. But then the awful news came, and now Chief Petty Officer Charles Ross Pettit's name appears on the list of casualties the Arizona suffered on that day. Ross's Dad, Uncle Roy, Mom's brother, came for visits afterward, and he was still a kind, tall, handsome, likable uncle, but after Pearl Harbor, his face was never again quite the same. It seemed darker to me than it was before the war, and I felt the unacknowledged pain of the loss that hovered over us all. I often now wonder if later Fifth Marine brother, Sergeant Leonard, and Army Tank Corps Sergeant Lavon, who sat at table with Ross in '41, fondly recalled that wonderful August night with Ross as they passed through Honolulu on the way to their battle stations.

What Ross's visit shows above all is that we never knew when a seemingly accidental surprise and joyful visit might later gain such a weighty importance. Even the faintest intimation of that possibility served to take our minds off our farm-induced weariness and to teach us in the most basic way what is really important in life. The role that food and the mealtime played in that Depression setting to relieve the burden of grinding poverty and to ritualize celebratory moments is hard to overestimate. Before one meal had ended, we were always looking forward to the next. The meal did so much more than fuel hungry, needy bodies. I am struck by the relative paucity of attention given to the farm mealtime in the Great Depression in a large and recent volume on food history offered by the prestigious Oxford University Press.* We turn now to consider another way we coped with the stresses laid on Arkansas farm families by the Great Depression, namely the way play had a magical or almost miraculous therapeutic value.

---

* See *The Oxford Handbook of Food History*, ed. Jeffrey M. Pilcher (New York: Oxford University Press, 2012).

Chapter 5

Play

THE SEPARATE TREATMENTS of work and play during the Great Depression are artificial, for they were a seamless and nourishing whole, but for the sake of discussion, I separate them here. Play unites all living, thinking, feeling creatures—human and nonhuman, young and old, male and female. All alike play, and in play a beam of transcendence shines through; in play creatures secure a bond with other creatures and transcend the boring and ordinary. Pain from work and injury is soothed, and community is celebrated. The mere existence of play schools, play therapy, play studies, and play practice all affirm play as a core value.

1. Childhood Play

The folk adage that work without play deadens was simply taken for granted by my Depression family. Our farm rituals and schedules of play brought relief from fatigue and renewal for the next week's challenges. It offered weekend and rainy day respites, and the after-supper recess from work joined us youngish souls with kinfolk and locals on the dirt road out front to play hide and seek in the dark, to flirt, to chase fire flies, to play Red Rover, and to let out screams of delight piercing the darkness.

Saturday afternoons, Sundays, and rainout days also opened doors to play. We boys would rush off to skinny-dip in the "hole" on

Glaise Creek, a ten-minute walk away. There, all of the boys learned to swim and loved to bomb (drop on) other swimmers as we swung from the loose vine over the swimming hole, to splash older brothers, and to be ducked and splashed in turn. Coming out of the Ozark foothills a mile away, the Glaise Creek water was cool and clean enough for swimming even in steamy-hot July or August. Wanda and I also pedaled our bikes to Nelson's hole in the hills, which was cool, clear, deep, and *free*. There she learned to swim, and I developed my skill.

Also special interactive playtimes delighted my sister and me. When we were preschoolers, our play almost drove our mother crazy. There was the day when, to conquer our boredom, we decided to climb the very large century-old red oak tree across the road in front of the house. It posed a challenge. Its girth was so large that we could not hug it to shinny up to the first limb, but undeterred, we climbed the smaller hickory beside it, crossed over into the mother oak on an outstretched branch, then picked our way fifty feet higher to the top of the oak. A fall from that height would have injured or killed one or both of us. Disturbed by our quietness, Mom came into the front yard and called and then heard our wimpy answers from the top of the oak. Rather than fainting on the spot, screaming alarm, or yelling for our dad's help, she wisely and calmly announced dinner. "You can come down now," she said. Once our feet were firmly and safely planted on the earth, she shook us both and gave one of her angriest lectures; those special lectures were sobering and memorable. She made us promise never, ever to do that again. Though what we did was fun to us, we did admit that it was a little bit scary. We loved it and called it fun, but true to our promise, we never did it again. The memory of that frightening experience helps me now understand why young and old actively seek the thrills of hang gliding, bungee jumping, skydiving, and mountain climbing.

We once committed another prank that we forever lamented. One can understand our reasoning. We had to pump water for the thirsty animals, and seeing their large, hollow, cypress trough filled with cool, clean water gave us an idea. We had seen dogs Rack and Buddy swim in creeks and lakes, but we had never seen a cat swim.

We thought the cats needed a lesson. To force the issue, we captured the cats living under the house in a burlap bag and then released them one by one into the trough of water. They resisted mightily; they scratched, bit, meowed, and protested with all their might. Yet we stubbornly continued a tutoring that inflicted fright, pain, and mortal harm on some of the cats. That sick gesture brought a stern lecture from *both* parents *and* brothers. The scratches on our bare arms advertised our guilt, and that little ugly game showed us the dark side of play. In the taunts, bullying, and teasing that school-mates heaped on others, we later saw how hurtful those dark, "play-ful" acts can be.

Such a shadow side of play came in another childhood incident that still causes me pain. Although she was younger by over a year, Wanda was a better athlete than I. Her maturation was ahead of mine, and she was quicker and better coordinated than I. In our staged races, she would always win, but I kept trying, hoping to improve. In one of our little racing games, she, as usual, took the lead and was far enough ahead to scamper up the catalpa tree in the yard to elude my tag. In her climbing haste, she slipped and fell to the ground, badly hurt. For weeks I was shamed when I saw my right-handed soul mate awkwardly trying to feed herself with her left hand because her favored right arm was cased in plaster.

There is evidence on my body as well that she could inflict pain as well as suffer it. There is still a large scar on the back of my right forearm from a wound from her pushing me backward onto a hoe. My right wrist also still bears a C-shaped scar from a game of car racing with bottles on our homemade dirt track. Her race car passed mine, swished in front, and with its broken neck, sliced into my wrist to eliminate me as a competitor. Those mishaps, however, were few; our play was mostly joyful, and it nourished a lifelong bond.

Into summer and winter schedule cracks, we inserted moments of play that liberated and delighted. We played hopscotch, shot marbles, chased fireflies, joined in games of hide-and-seek, and led friends in matches of tag in the hay in the barn loft and in the tops of a cluster of nearby trees. On occasion we caught baseballs Daddy hit to us in the pasture. On winter evenings, we played Chinese checkers and cards, and in midwinter cold, we skated on ice-covered ponds with our street shoes.

Our teamwork, sometimes aided by our parents, produced a culinary delight. I was nine and Wanda was seven. We had seen the brothers build and use a screened seine to catch crayfish in a local pond to use as bait to snag perch in the creek nearby. We had the idea that it would be more efficient just to eat the crayfish tails ourselves and not use them as bait in an intermediate step. Mom aided our crazy scheme by loaning us a small skillet, bagging some flower with a bit of grease, helping us select kindling, and providing us matches. She may have thought our idea was so foolish, it would never materialize, but if she so thought, she was mistaken. In spite of her idle doubts, we had good luck with the seining, and soon we had enough crayfish for a meal. After out catch, we removed the tails, peeled the little creatures, kindled a fire, then cooked and ate our catch on the bank of the pond. The memory of the taste of those succulent morsels still makes my mouth water. The recall of that unscripted moment of spontaneous play still twitches the corners of my lips up into a smile, but it also saddens. The pond is now so polluted, no one would dare eat its fare.

Nature's surprises often triggered other play opportunities. Our farmhouse sat on a small knoll, and below it and nearby, a branch ran through the farm. A bridge spanned the branch to permit crossing to Uncle's house during the rainy season. During overflows the water snaked through our pasture to feed the branch. When that occurred, Wanda and I would spend hours folding school paper into small boats and launching them from the little wooden bridge. We dug empty bottles and lids out of the trash and wrote and stuffed messages inside to imaginary friends: "Wherever you find this, write me at . . ." Of course, no answer ever came, but the act itself stoked fertile childhood imaginings and fueled a capacity that endured. Those little surprises of liberation from sharing the farm workload were just plain fun, fun, fun, and they refreshed our little bodies for the return of the work regimen.

2. Liberating Family Play

There were times also when play engaged and refreshed the entire family and offered a respite from our onerous, grimy, toil-filled days. During spring and early summer, we were almost frenetically involved in planting, tilling, thinning, and weeding tasks, and the rise of hot, steamy, humid air from the dark earth reddened our faces and caused the sweat to roll.

By July the planting, cultivating, and weeding were complete, and the crops "laid by." By then our bodies cried out for relief from the oppressive hundred-degree heat from earth's oven. The pause from hard, sweaty tasks allowed for a family recess. On the Fourth of July, we almost always were free to make homemade ice cream—a rich, creamy, delicious fruit-flavored peach, strawberry, or blackberry delicacy. From the hundred-pound block of ice bought and stored in the porch wooden icebox, we crushed enough and mixed it with salt for our wooden hand-cranked freezer to convert the liquid into a yummy dessert. Wanda and I were allowed to take turns at the crank and then were rewarded with the first serving from the freezer canister. When darkness came on the fourth, we would set off a few firecrackers or sparklers, much to the dismay of dog Rack.

Connected with this lay-by break came a long-weekend family fishing trip and picnic on the nearby White River. Typically, Daddy, Uncle, and I launched the event. We loaded Daddy's jon boat onto the truck and filled it with trotlines, seines, paddles, tarp, cooking gear, groceries, a few cane fishing poles, old quilts for sleeping, and a wooden fish box for the catch. Once at the river, we seined minnows for bait, set and baited trotlines, made camp, stoked a fire, and took a skinny-dip from the Dexter bar. After a supper of roasted homemade brats, we sat by the fire as darkness fell and the heavens beamed, offering a luminescent display of the Big Dipper and Milky Way and delightful views of fiery meteoroids, or "shooting stars," streaking to earth. I can still hear the hoots of night owls near and far and the screams of the screech owl piercing the thick darkness. After a night of sleep on the ground, we rose at first light to run the trotlines and drop the catch of catfish, buffalo, and drum into our live box. A breakfast of fried potatoes, homemade bread, slab bacon, and eggs cooked over an open fire launched our day and kept the mosquitoes away.

In that breakfast circle, I could eavesdrop on conversations that Uncle and Daddy never had anywhere else. How long ago, they wondered, did the river change its course from its Party Creek path near the homeplace? How faraway was the full moon last night—you think, it looked so close? Is there anything we can do for Mamma (my grandma), whose health is failing? What can we do about the bootleggers stealing our corn for moonshine? Could the county sheriff help us, you think? Where did the eels come from that are now found in the river? And Uncle would wink at me and say, "Isn't this fun, Toon? Someday I won't be able to do this anymore. Hurry up and become a doctor so when I get sick, you can fix me up."

The river setting worked miracles; we were so at ease that one night out seemed to cure the strain of weeks and weeks of hard, sweaty labor. In the morning's early light on the river, the world seemed more friendly and beautiful. For a child to share that experience and to eavesdrop on the depth, richness, understanding, and genuine affection between these two brothers was a beautiful thing. I now realize how rare and precious that experience was.

Recalling now how death cut the cord binding those brothers and closed the ledger on those sacred moments still saddens. When my father died on the kitchen floor at home from a heart attack twenty-five years later, Uncle was heartbroken. The memory of the pain Wanda felt as she and midwife cousin Edith failed to revive him is still fresh, and the awful moment when she delivered the news to Uncle is as vivid as yesterday. In the frantic aftermath, Uncle, my dad's senior, was a major worry, for his heart had been failing for years. Being six years older, he expected and wanted to die first.

Hoping to avoid staging two funerals at once, we took Uncle to the Dr. for an examination. We needed assurance that it was safe for him to attend the service. After carefully moving his stethoscope over Uncle's bare old black-haired chest, he paused for a moment to think, then the physician carefully and gently offered, "Mr. Roetzel, I do not think it wise for you to attend your brother's funeral. If he were alive, he would not want you to risk your life to honor him. You can honor him in lots of other ways." Uncle paused for a moment to absorb the news and reflect, and then in his quiet, almost inaudible voice, he said, "Doc, I am very sorry. I cannot take your advice. I'm goin'; I just gotta go."

He dressed up in a suit and attended the service in the local Methodist Church, sobbing from beginning to end; when he walked by the open casket at the front of the sanctuary, his body shook, and he stooped over, patted Daddy's chest, and said, "Goodbye, Bub." It is hardly surprising that he also died in his sleep just a bit over a year later. After he lost the most precious person in the world to him, there was no need to go on; his life also ended when Dad left him behind. Our river overnight camping and the next day's picnic showed me something so rare that even now it seems almost a sacrilege to have viewed it and now to share it.

Uncle John, Aunt Minnie, Melanie, Mom, Wanda, and Lavon would soon join our little threesome. They came bouncing across the field on its dirt path in Uncle's John's 1938 Dodge pickup—Aunt Minnie sat in the cab, and the rest were seated in the truck bed. The emerging riverside fish fry picnic, swimsuit dips from the river sandbar, and search for turtle eggs set loose a frenzy of excitement. As we little ones raced about, looking for turtle eggs, Wanda rushed to tell me that she had learned to "potty on the ground." As a child, I did not understand the gender-role shift that the river placed on Daddy, Uncle, and Uncle John. The men did the cooking over the open fire and the cleanup. It was a beautiful moment, for it allowed Mom and Aunt Minnie a little vacation from their unending, monotonous chores.

This refreshing, playful pause did many things. It marked an important transition in the farm calendar; it celebrated family connections and our place in a beautiful, generous, and physically pleasing natural setting. It marked our childhood calendar; after this break, our school summer session always opened. This early start allowed for a fall break so children could later vacation to pick cotton. There were fishing opportunities in spring and fall that allowed for short one-day trips, but none could compare with the Fourth of July river treat.

Those outings and play recesses cemented ties between old and young, parents and children, male and female and were always energizing. This awareness remained with me when I served as an Air Force chaplain in the fifties on the DEW (Distance Early Warning) Line in the Arctic, riding with bush pilots from radar site to site. With my Bible and prayer book, I always carried a fishing pole. My tour of duty, like that of the airmen, was fifteen months. I travelled constantly, seven days a week, from site to site for short three-day stays. I would take care of emergencies, hold services, teach a class, counsel those needing help, and visit local Inuit tribes. In that time, I had several narrow escapes and logged more miles in fifteen months than the circuit rider John Wesley did in a lifetime. But the time was rich, and the need was great. After all of those months of isolation, some young airmen would start to crack emotionally. If I noticed anyone with a heavy, leaden look, I would single him out (all males in the nineteen fifties) and suggest that we go fishing or, if it were winter, that we take a walk. The therapeutic value of such an outing, even in minus-forty-degree weather, was undeniable whether on the Yukon or Snake Rivers or on the coast of the Bering Sea. Those outings lifted spirits, theirs and mine, and relieved tensions. I saw new interest in peers and the world around emerge and others stepping in to lead outings. There was a palpable value of such play or fun episodes; the benefits were very much like those of my family in the Great Depression, where play was a necessary survival skill.

On the Arkansas farm, the Great Depression lasted for a very long time, and lives were cut short by the stress. Some think that the results of the Great Depression still linger in the lower life expectancy of the state's residents, its lowered annual family income (2016 barely one-half of that of Maryland), and its lower-than-average college-graduation rates. Studies have shown that in the rural South, the Depression began soon after WWI and continued until after World War II, and its effects still linger. In 1933, after FDR was elected president, he sought and gained congressional support for the Rural Electrification Agency (REA), and that program aimed to provide needed assistance for poor, rural areas, but it took fifteen years for those valuable power lines to reach our farm. Millions of other rural poor were caught in the vicious economic and social catastrophe that in the White River Delta region was more severe than other parts of the country. Play offered an antidote for the pain, depression, and loneliness imposed by those burdens, and it awakened in our souls an "ode to joy" that bound us all in a common life-sustaining lump. But in my little young mind, those joys did not eradicate the deep and abiding sense that "we wuz poor" nor of the special limits on life and its fulfillment that that poverty imposed.

My family always found release from an oppressive work schedule in games. In winter months, my dad and I often played checkers after supper. Sometimes he would let me win, but the most special joy came when I won because I outwitted him. Most of our family games cost little, if anything. Tied to the great oak across the road from the house was a great bag swing and a perch from which we could launch. Next to that were two pegs marking the limits of our "horseshoe" game. (The name *horseshoe* was a misnomer, for we played with discarded mule shoes that were smaller and cost-free.) In the backyard, we fashioned and attached a broken metal and wooden barrel hoop to the smokehouse for our faux basketball practice and games. Instead of a real leather-clad basketball, we played with a large, round rubber child's ball. We shared ball gloves that we exchanged for makeup games of baseball and softball games. No wonder that in that environment, competing daily with older brothers, Wanda would grow up to be the best athlete in the family. In high school, she would play shortstop on three county softball championships. All of the older brothers also played on championship teams, but her numbers were superior.

3. School Sports

As I now reflect on that Depression legacy, I wonder why teams like ours, with players from farm families and from small high schools in small towns, could be so tough and competitive. Our teams had little coaching, inferior facilities, and little practice time, yet we persisted. The boys' softball teams, like the girls', could not afford uniforms or spiked shoes. We played in blue jeans, T-shirts, and tennis shoes or even bare feet. Heat in our gymnasium for our basketball games came from a single wood stove, and the gym had no indoor toilets or showers for players. All coaches taught full-time and coached on the side. We were hauled to games by parents in their cars or in the bed of a truck. Did those handicaps spur us on against more advantaged teams from larger schools with modern facilities? Were our efforts attempts to prove that we were not inferior? Did that spur us to excel and to fill the trophy case with our awards? I am still unsure how to answer those questions.

There was certainly excitement that came with winning, but one of the great benefits of those games was the development of motor skills, a team spirit, and community recognition. Although there were excellent teams, one of the things that we all learned from that play environment was how to lose. It was not that we were forever "losers," but when a loss came, as it inevitably did, we learned how to accept and learn from that experience and to rise to compete another day.

Sister Wanda played shortstop on three county softball championship teams and on one championship basketball team. She was tiny but quick, and there were two larger young women who carried the basketball team to victory after victory. After the girls' basketball championship one year, it was assumed that with many of the same players returning, they would repeat. The year looked promising as the team continued to win. Then in the county tournament, the team easily advanced to the finals. In the championship game, Wanda's team was leading by six points, with three minutes to play, and we were already sensing another championship was ours. But then something happened that was painful to watch and now to remember. The opponent recovered and went ahead by two points with five seconds to go. Sister Wanda made a drive for the basket with time expiring, and just before the final whistle was fouled in the act of shooting, her shot went in, but the referee ruled that it came after the game-ending whistle. Now, everything rested on those two free throws. We thought she could do it; she dribbled nervously at the free throw line then shot her first of two; the first went in, and now her team was down by just one. If she could tie the game, we just knew her team would win in overtime. Hers, I was convinced, was the superior team. But the second shot, though more accurate than the first, hit the back of the rim and bounced away. Her team lost. Through tears I hugged her later, but that did not ease her pain. We slept in separate rooms at home that night. And through the wall, I could hear her sobs; I still can feel her pain and the frustration of my faltering efforts to comfort her. "*I* lost it," she said. I hugged her with all my might, and she knew I was with her, win or lose. After a night of some sleep, she arose the next morning to go to school and to face the new day's challenges as a strong young woman. That experience is common to all who play sports; in playing games, we learned how to lose and to rise again to fight. Thus, our participation in sports during the Great Depression tutored us in important survival skills. We did have successes, I fewer than other family members, but we all experienced losses, and in coping with those loses, we were taught to face adversity with grace, honesty, and resolve. That was a valuable lesson not just for surviving in the Great Depression but for all of life and all professions. That lesson saved our lives, and through it a new resolve and solidarity was forged.

When we did win, the whole community celebrated our little championships. There were free dinners, community praise in the stores, and a shared sense of importance. When we lost in the finals, there was support and encouragement. No one in the small community ever smirked or called us losers.

Wanda, whose teams were the best, also played on teams that lost at critical moments. It is no wonder that after completing her junior college degree, she was hired to teach in a small rural school near Toad Suck Ferry and found the strength after a hard week of work to enroll in a weekend degree program at Arkansas State Teachers' College. Our pusher Mom ordered me to drive out from Hendrix College each Saturday morning in my old red 1948 Ford pickup to ferry her to and from her weekend classes. The heroic example she set for students from desperately poor homes inspired young girls especially. She modeled a behavior they could strive to emulate.

Finally, in our Great Depression family, play had many other broader functions. It joined the human to the nonhuman world, it offered rest and refreshment from the fatigue of a survival modus operandi, it brought release and self-transcendence, it strengthened personal bonds, it enhanced mental and physical strength and stamina, and it taught resilience. Play for us had an almost mystical, if not magical, value that I have tried to capture in the lines below:

Play as the Soul's Music

O creatures at play you still bring joy to the boy
I was then.
The mules lope out, kick up both heels and bray.
The dogs wrestle, growl, and play-bite their mates.
The piglets grunt, and romp, and squeal.
The kittens roll, and scratch, and paw;
They do not mean to injure though.
The calves butt heads, and race about.
The birds loud flutter, dart, and squawk.
The fish leaps high, and arcs back home.
The baby crayfish race the pond.
We kids play tag in tree and barn.
And all alike do hide and seek.
Play joins us all in nature's choir for an "Ode to Joy."

Chapter 6

Homecoming

AFTER THE NORMANDY Landing on June 6, 1944, the tide of World War II shifted. Before that epochal moment, we could not be certain that the Allied armies would emerge victorious. With that tidal shift, our hopes soared. Almost eleven months later (May 7, 1945), Germany surrendered, and we knew Franklin, then in France, would soon be home again. We worried, however, about the two brothers in the Pacific. News of Leonard's Marine unit in red-hot combat on Iwo Jima terrified us, and reports that Lavon's flame-throwing tank brigade was facing fierce resistance from die-hard fighters further darkened our fears.

Between 1940 and 1942, we stood in front of our house to bid those three farewell as they left for war. Rare were the occasions when I recall seeing my father spontaneously and unashamedly weep. One such occasion came during the war in 1945 as we followed the struggle of Leonard's Fifth Marine Division to capture and control Iwo Jima, a weigh station for the anticipated invasion of Japan. The early radio broadcasts about the invasion, beginning in February, predicted a short and decisive campaign, but weeks passed with no resolution. The report of stubborn Japanese resistance continued, and the campaign went on and on. We soon learned the causality rate was high, very high, at almost 50 percent of the entire Fifth. In that campaign, US losses exceeded even those of the defending Japanese forces. The campaign for Iwo finally was declared over in March, after almost three months, not the two weeks of fighting predicted. Even after we heard that Iwo had fallen, weeks and weeks passed with no word from Leonard. Wanda and I trudged to the mailbox daily, only to traipse home empty-handed. We had given up hope and assumed the worst. We all dreaded the awful moment when an envelope would come from the secretary of defense, beginning, "We regret to inform you." The wait for word, any word, was excruciating. We would have welcomed even word that he was recovering in a hospital, but nothing came. Only eight weeks later, when we made our Saturday trip to Russell to buy groceries, did our story have a resolution. Arriving in town, we stopped as usual by the post office in an off chance we would hear something, and we came face-to-face with *the* decisive moment. We pulled up to the curb at the local Russell office, and the postmaster cousin came running out with a letter held high and handed it to my dad, still sitting in the truck. Dad saw that it was from Leonard, and even before he opened that letter, he wept uncontrollably. His body shook with sobs. Minutes later, after he recovered a bit, he carefully and slowly opened the small envelope with his pocketknife to learn Leonard *had* not only survived the Iwo struggle, but he was also uninjured. As a sharpshooter who had seen fierce combat, his survival was a miracle. He was writing, however, from Hawaii, where the Fifth was training with the Second for the expected imminent invasion of Japan. After receiving that letter, none of us could later remember what else we did in town that day. Dad drove home slowly, knowing that one of the three red stars hanging in our front window would not be turning to gold, at least not yet. We desperately hoped we would not become a "gold-star family."

From the national news, however, we had no access to information about Lavon's tank unit. And not knowing was painful beyond words. We did know he was involved in combat, and from Leonard's experience, we knew the resistance was formidable. For weeks the struggle continued to take Japanese-controlled islands; it seemed to last forever. We read of suicidal kamikaze attacks on American ships and troop formations, and we knew resistance even more fierce could be expected in an invasion of the Japanese mainland. That fear robbed our mealtimes of conversation and laughter. We ate in silence as the summer wore on.

The report of the August 6 atomic bombing of Hiroshima and Nagasaki gave us hope that the end was finally near, but word that those frightful weapons snuffed out the lives of over one hundred thousand noncombatants saddened. When Japan surrendered just days later, our deep sleep returned. Even at fourteen, I noticed the toll the worry took on my parents; both remembered the poison gas horrors of WWI. They knew that war *is* hell. "They are so young," my dad muttered. "I wish I could have gone in their place." New creases wrinkled his brow. Mom's erect posture sagged; her hair thinned, and the easy smile went limp. A somber mood hung like a dark cloud over mealtimes. But news of the war's end lightened our spirits; smiles returned, and anticipations of the boys' return spawned joyful anticipation.

After his six-year absence, the image of Franklin's homecoming is still as vivid as yesterday. On a Saturday afternoon, in August of 1945, we loaded into the Dodge pickup for our weekly grocery run. Uncle and I sat on the metal floor of the bed with our backs to the cab. A crate holding thirty dozen freshly washed eggs, to be used for barter at thirty cents a dozen, was at our feet, and two fifty-pound sacks of potatoes going for $4 each rested to the side. In the cab were Mom and Dad and Titter in the middle.

As the engine started, I glimpsed a smallish figure on our dirt road a quarter of a mile away. I stood up for a better view, and there was a uniformed figure limping toward home. Once I saw that right-legged limp from an old childhood injury from schoolyard bullies, I knew it was Franklin. Thumping on the cab, I screamed and shouted over and over: "It's Franklin, it's Franklin, it's Franklin, it's Franklin; he's home agin!" The truck emptied instantly, and we stood in the middle of the road, jumping up and down, waving, screaming, and yelling. Franklin dropped his duffel and ran to join us. After six long years, he was home again. The tears of joy flowed freely; we hugged and hugged and hugged again. Uncle embraced Franklin and then slipped away to spread the news. Within an hour, Aunt Minnie, Uncle John, and cousin Melanie came rushing through the pasture.

Grandma, who bade her little Liebling goodbye in 1940, was no longer with us, and military duty had kept Franklin from her funeral in 1942. We keenly felt her absence but imagined her smiling down on this great reunion.

We celebrated all afternoon and into the night. The questions tumbled out; we chattered nonstop. Then came the special joy of the magical homecoming ritualistic meal Mom rushed to prepare. At her Home Comfort altar in her floppy, loose-fitting, faded, robe-like dress, she threw a pan of rising dough into a hot, hot wood-fired oven. Time flew, and soon a pan of six brown-crusted loaves came out. Franklin took a hot loaf, sliced off the heel, lathered it with freshly churned butter, and devoured a delicacy he had not tasted for six years in the Air Corps NCO mess. Then he cut a thick slice off the loaf, soaked it with soup bean liquid and bacon drippings, and wolfed that down as well. Ironically, this preference of his would later become a favorite of daughter Becky. When we sat at the table with the whole crowd, he had the first pick from the fried-chicken platter; he took the drumstick that I preferred, but it didn't matter; he was home again. With the crusty chicken thighs came scalloped fried-potatoes, thick slices of beef steak tomatoes, spinach, and cucumbers, and to cap it all off, out of the oven came a hot peach cobbler. The memory of that joyous, almost sacramental moment still lingers.

After the weekend celebration, Franklin said to me, "Let's take a little ride." I was too happy to ask, "Where we goin'"? After we loaded, he drove straight to Bald Knob seven miles away and parked in front of Huffakers store. He asked a clerk for jackets for boys then fitted and bought me a child's leather pilot's jacket. I loved that jacket and wore it until it was tattered and too tight for comfort. It recalled a great moment. My second Daddy who was gone was home again, alive and caring.

After Japan's surrender, rejoicing continued nonstop as Leonard and Nanny Lavon returned; we were so happy. Life was good. For the first time in over six years, seven heads circled the dinner table; the red stars in the window marking their service came down. It was heaven on earth. Being a curious teenager, I was alive with questions about their war experience, but the brothers were not eager to rehearse that painful chapter. Recalling those horrific moments was just too painful, and they would not pick at the psychic sores the war left.

Only much later in life, I caught them with Dad and tried once more to encourage them to share their war experiences. They stubbornly rejected any such suggestion. Even years later, they refused to recall those nightmarish horrors. I tried another tact. I asked if they would share some funny stories from the war experience. Dad was the first to begin the cycle. It was early in 1918, he noted, and his unit of ammunition carriers was on the way to the front in France. With his farm experience, he had been assigned to a unit with a full complement of mules to lug heavy, explosive munitions to the front in wagons. The mules were trained to tolerate loud noises and to serve as a team. What Dad remembered was a funny event that may have saved his life. On the ocean voyage to France, his unit's men were all placed in the ship with their animals so that they could clean up after, feed, water, and curry them. Smart, right? But in someone's misplaced wisdom, all of the harness, collars, lines, tow chains, ammo, *and* wagons were loaded onto another ship. And guess, he asked, which ship was torpedoed by the Germans. Everyone burst with laughter. Then he spoke of the weeks it took to gather the necessary equipment in France to harness the mules and to confiscate wagons to move the munitions. Those torpedoes, he noted, "probably saved my life. And the mules were happy too."

Then Franklin had a lifesaving story of his own. During the Normandy invasion, his unit was to drop the 101st airborne paratrooper unit behind the German lines to offer cover and protection for the troops storming the beaches. There would be two major moves on succeeding days. On June 6, the day of the invasion, the drop would take place, and on the next day, flights would drop supplies to the 101st. Franklin was to go on one flight, and a partner would take the other. They drew straws to see who would go first on what was expected to be a dangerous mission. Franklin drew the short straw and had to go with the drop on June 6. By the next day, the German defenses were ready, and his buddy who drew the long straw perished when his plane was shot down. Survival, he noted, was not about skill; it was about luck. To this story about luck, he too added a funny one.

He and a good buddy desperately wanted to go to London for a taste of the sights and high life even during the bombings, but they were frustrated at every turn. Somehow, they figured out a way to steal the captain's jeep on a weekend, to fill it with fuel and drive to London in the dark of night with mandated dimmed lights. They felt so smug, but an army MP in London was suspicious. He confronted them and found they had no vehicle permit or orders authorizing their visit. He confiscated the jeep, temporarily detained them, and filed a report for disciplinary action. It could have been really, really bad. They faced possible demotion, even some brig time or, horror of horrors, a dishonorable discharge. But they had enough "brownie points" and were needed badly enough to be spared by their commanding officer. The major, nevertheless, did extract a vow that they would never, ever to do such a crazy thing again. From then on, they were confined to the area, and their only contact with the outside world was to hand out rationed gum and candy to neighborhood children. They did meet some interesting young women that way. An aside: in 1990 I met the postmaster in the little town nearby, and unbelievably, he was one of those befriended children given candy by GIs like my brother, if not by him personally.

Leonard's story was the funniest of all. Not only was he a sharpshooter and on duty, he was also a trained cook for his company. After weeks of the struggle to take Iwo Jima, he had the crazy idea that he would try to improve morale by serving his entire company pancakes for breakfast. The problem was he had no cooktops. His master sergeant managed, however, to requisition (military jargon for *steal*) cooktops en route to an army unit. With those stoves, Leonard and his helpers cooked whole-wheat pancakes for over three hundred men in his company. He was right; that act did improve morale. Dad, Lavon, and Franklin just exploded in laughter, and all understood that story's rationale totally. Lavon joked in jest, "Then if you were so great, why weren't you commissioned a first lieutenant on the spot?" More laughter. That was all I was allowed to hear.

As blissful as was this homecoming, the heavenly moment was clouded by a dark shadow. Not all boys who left to fight came home. Their memory was and still is fresh. We could not help but remember Chief Petty Officer Charles Ross Pettit, mom's beloved and only nephew, whose life was snatched away in the Pearl Harbor bombings of '41. He is now memorialized on the list of casualties the Arizona took that day. Dorothy, Leonard's sweetheart and wife-to-be, lost brother Wayne Clinton Johnson in the battle for Saipan in 1944. Her parents nursed the Purple Heart he won but carried the painful burden of that loss the rest of their lives. Dorothy, like so many others, mourned her beloved brother, and as she watched us celebrate, she surely secretly asked what-if questions. What would it really be like if Wayne were here? What would be his favorite foods? Who would he be courting to marry? And so on.

Once all of the boys were home, courtships deferred for years blossomed again, and by 1948 the family circle expanded as brothers exchanged vows, "till death do us part," with three wonderful women—Franklin to Beulah, Leonard to Dorothy, and Lavon to Lois. The time was euphoric, but for me that moment could not last. My high school graduation would soon separate me at sixteen from that blissful scene. Life on the farm in the Great Depression was unimaginably hard, but there was a certain security in knowing what real and imagined challenges we faced. The unknown path ahead frightened me more. It was fraught with the peril of not knowing what risks it concealed. I was frightened, insecure, and to borrow W. H. Auden's phrase, was "all on edge." Where would life's pathway lead?

The stress I felt came partly from the acceleration of the growth process spurred by my family's Great Depression survival struggles. Our intermediate adolescent period of questioning, sorting, rebellion, challenging authority, stolid silences, and cynicism was snatched from us. We had no time to learn whom and what to trust. Wanda's childhood and mine ended when all of the brothers went off to war; although still children, we instantly stepped into adult roles. The dizziness that acceleration caused may explain the fears I had of the next step. We were adults before we were ready to be adults. What would happen, I wondered, when I graduated from high school in the spring of 1948? I had no idea what I was saying when I read the Longfellow line the superintendent scripted for me in my graduation address: "Lives of all great men [it was *men*] remind us; we too can make out lives sublime." And so on.

With every reason to be joyful, one other issue intruded to disturb. With some of the added income from the war years now available, my parents decided to make the move my mother had wanted for twenty years. The new location on a farm plot just a half mile away was on the main road and offered an unobstructed view of the beautiful Ozark foothills. I helped my dad collect rocks from those hills for the foundation; I assisted with the laying of the foundation. I pounded nails in the framing, painted the sheetrock, wired the new house with the help of a friend, and helped plumb the new structure. For the first time ever, we were soon to have the electricity FDR promised in 1933. We had three bedrooms, running water, an indoor toilet, and a view of the Ozarks that transported.

This should have been a really exciting time for me, but something in me held back. Now I realize Lawrence Durel was right. We *are* creatures of our landscape. This comfortable new place was not home. The old board-and-batten unpainted farmhouse and the large barn sided with long white oak planks eighteen inches wide with stalls for the animals, and the large hayloft where we played still called me. The privileged large stall on the barn's end once housed mule Bud, a dear friend and tutor who saved my life. His bones still lie in the corner pasture. Protector dog Rack's remains lay in the corner of the farmyard by the mulberry tree. The outbuildings—corncrib, chicken house, smokehouse, and cotton shed—that once bustled with life now stood empty but still summoned. There was the corncrib where once I grew a bit in the remorse I felt for shooting a sparrow for fun. There was the hand pump where my little arm went up and down rhythmically to water the animals. There I brought Dickie in from the pasture, and there Wanda and I climbed the great oak in front of the house. There were the orchard and garden that fed us and the blackberry vines whose luscious fruit Wanda and I picked. There we played, screamed, and chased fireflies. The new house was convenient, comfortable, warm, and attractive, but my soul was elsewhere.

Even though I recognized my mother's need for more social inter-action and her craving for a beautiful aesthetically pleasing view, I could not deny the physical and psychological dislocation I felt in the new place. The dislocation I felt compounded the dread I felt that my after–high school future imposed.

The question is now moot, for neither house remains except in my memory and in the stories that give those memories life. The new house stood empty after Mom died in 1966, then some crooked spirits broke into the house and illegally cooked methamphetamines that burned it to the ground. The old homeplace that I have crudely sketched below was reduced to ashes by a grassfire out of control. The fire also took the barn, garage, corncrib, chicken house, smoke-house, cotton shed, and even the outhouse; it also claimed the out-buildings and house of Grandma, from whom I learned the meaning of grace, and Uncle, who served as a grandpa substitute for us. Only the stories that remain cannot be burned. If one grants that stories are memory keepers, guardians of a past, teachers of the present, and the architects of an open future, the ashes of the buildings and the old farmyard jonquils once lining the path to the front porch that still come up and bloom in the spring help keep the story alive.

Chapter 7

Quo Vadis: An Afterword

IN A TIME when many see immigrants as a threat to America's stability, prosperity, and quality of life, I offer the following biographical sketches as counterevidence.

Franklin (1918–1994) was in the Army Air Corps from 1940–1945 and engaged in the Normandy invasion and occupation force. With help from the GI Bill, he completed a master's degree in Arkansas history, taught, coached, and served as a school principal in Bald Knob for a total of over thirty years. He helped integrate his school without incident. He served as Sunday school teacher, public servant, and caregiver for aging parents and Uncle, father of daughters Becky and Fran. He was a devoted husband to Beulah, who was one of the best cooks in the family, and helped make the world a better place.

Leonard (1923–2001) was a sergeant in the Marine Corp's Fifth Division on Iwo Jima, 1945. He was a mentor and model, smart with a sense of humor. He was a sportsman and proud father and grandfather and served as a house parent, counselor, and mentor to young boys in a correctional facility in Woodburn, Oregon. His children are Vicky and Larry. He was independent, loving, and forceful. He did some college work and will be forever missed.

Nanny Lavon (1924–2003) was a tank corps army sergeant in combat in WWII 1944–1945. He fought in Pacific Theater. He has an AA degree from Beebe Junior College. He was a career lineman and technician for the Bell system. He was an honest, loving, compassionate, and giving Nanny for infants Wanda and me, and he entertained wide circle of friends and family with his dry wit. His children (Mike and Linda) and grandchildren also found his skimpy, boney lap to be a safe place. He made the world and his immediate neighborhood a more joyful place. The laughter he inspired made many hearts glad.

Sister Wanda, Titter to us (1933–2016) of the five children, has the strongest case for sainthood. She was urged on to higher education by our mother, the Pusher. She served for over thirty years as fourth-grade elementary school teacher. Peers in the Arkansas educational system bestowed on her the accolade Teacher of the Year. She loved teaching fourth graders. She helped take down walls that divide peoples. She assisted with the first public school in Arkansas and local church integration. Friends, former students and their parents, and family filled the small church to pay respects at her farewell memorial service in December 2016 (see attachment). She and I came of age on an Arkansas farm in the Great Depression. She was tough, but with a contagious smile, her charity was unlimited. As the spouse to Chief Warrant Officer and highly decorated Army helicopter pilot Wayne, prisoner of the Korean War and with three tours in Vietnam, she served valiantly as a single-parent caregiver for daughter, Leta, when he was on foreign assignments. Generous, smart, athletic, and totally empathetic, she was a beloved grandma for three wonderful granddaughters, Alex, Anna, and Grace, of daughter, Leta. We shall not soon see the likes of her again.

Every fiber of my being was touched and informed by life with those siblings and my farm experience in the Great Depression. Urged on by great teachers and Pusher Mom, I had the benefit of a college, seminary, and graduate school education. After high school, there was only one acceptable answer to quo vadis. As valedictorian and salutatorian, friend Aubrey and I would both attend Beebe Junior College tuition-free. Established in 1927 before the Great Depression, the college purchased three school buses to be driven by students to ferry children of the poor to and from classes to earn an associate of arts college degree. Hopefully, that degree would open the door to further study. With the Beebe scholarship, room and board provided by our parents, and the cost of books, clothing, and classroom supplies earned by summer work and substitute bus driving, I earned my AA degree in the requisite two years, and Aubrey did so as well.

Beebe administrators hired young, able, idealistic ABD ("all but dissertation") faculty on the cheap to expand course offerings. Two of my best teachers ever were from that faculty. I think especially of my math teacher, Josephine Stone, to whom I later dedicated a book, and Mr. Clark, from whom I took courses in general chemistry and qualitative and quantitative analysis for my premed track. Ms. Stone pushed Aubrey and me in algebra, trigonometry, calculus, linear algebra, and geometry to the limit. We spent bus time collaborating on challenging math problems she assigned. As I neared the end of my second and last year at Beebe, Ms. Stone drew me aside and suggested that I consider applying for admission to MIT to do a math major. I had never heard of MIT, and the idea of moving so far away to attend college was terrifying and, I thought, financially impossible. I admit, though, that even though I was insecure and on edge, I was flattered, emboldened, and inspired by her sympathetic and supportive counsel. As I neared graduation, Dean Johnson summoned me to his office one day. I was terrified and wondered if I had wittingly or unwittingly committed a great no-no. I entered his office in a cold sweat. I could hardly believe the news he offered. Hendrix College was offering me a scholarship if I would enroll in the fall. The offer included a dining hall job to pay for my board. I was just transported and found enough voice to say yes on the spot. With summer work, my best friend Aubrey also found a way to join me, and we became roommates at that "reach" dream college, but sadly, his dreams of being a civil engineer were dashed when he was drafted out of college for service in the Korean conflict.

From Hendrix I went to seminary at Perkins School of Theology of SMU, where I really caught fire intellectually and met and married the love of my life, Caroline Kendall, with whom I have had sixty wonderful years. From that union came Lisa Caroline (1959, husband Alan Terraciano), Frank Werth (1961, Lisa Chandler),

Mary (1969), and grandson Anthony. Like every male member of my immigrant family, I served the country for three years in the Air Force as a military chaplain and then for seven years as a parish minister before the door opened for graduate study at Duke University (PhD, 1968) and thirty-five years as a professor of religious studies at Macalester College, St. Paul, five years at the University of Minnesota, and one at the University of Chicago, Divinity School. It may strike some readers as ironic that that service to community and country came from first- and second-generation descendants of immigrant families. Even though as a child, I knew we wuz poor, education, family support, great teachers, and habits of being learned in the Great Depression all combined with the nurture of a small church to foster a tradition of social service that inspired and lifted us all out of the clutches of poverty.

A final question intrudes: what remained from that Great Depression farm experience to inform and direct my forty-two years as a biblical scholar? First and foremost, because I knew that we wuz poor, I could easily identify and empathize with over 90 percent of the inhabitants of that ancient world. They too were poor. Most had roots in the soil; most struggled with issues of life and death, love and hate, defeat and triumph, hope and disappointment, life's darkness and light, and its high and low tides. Echoes from that past resonate in Jesus's special teaching, "Blessed are you poor for yours is the Kingdom of God" (Luke 6:20), and in the special indictment the prophets proclaim on those who turn aside from the needy (cf. Amos, Isaiah, Jeremiah, and the Proverbs).

The work habits that context imposed served me well in scholarship and teaching and helped me identify with and understand the inhabitants of the world I studied. Most were peasants tilling the soil or doing handwork. Even the great Apostle Paul shared that world as he made his living as a leather worker and tent maker.

The love I experienced there from family, nuclear and extended, and our animal friends helped me better understand how love is a source of strength and renewal inspiring observance of the commandment to serve God and neighbor. That experience helped me understand why the great Apostle Paul listed love as the greatest of all charismatic gifts—"faith, hope, love, abide, these three, but the greatest of them is love" (1 Corinthians 13:13, RSV). The episodes of storytelling I experienced there was not only central to my life as a scholar of old texts but also connected me to the cultural importance of stories as memory keepers of the lessons of world history.

My ties affirmed there of the interdependence of creature and creation sharpened my awareness of the inescapable linkage of the destiny of the human and natural world taken for granted in those old traditions (see especially Romans 8:20–25, where the fate of both is bound in a common bundle). Even while allowing for enormous differences, it takes little imagination to sense the secure tie binding the modern-to-some features of that ancient world.

To summarize this challenging and joyous journey, I call on the poem about Rabbi Ben Ezra written over a century ago by Robert Browning. I first encountered that poem in a literature course at Hendrix College on the front end of my academic pilgrimage. It begins as follows:

> Grow old along with me!
> The best is yet to be,
> The last of life, for which the first was made:
> Our times are in His hand
> Who saith "A whole I planned,
> Youth shows but half; trust God: see all, nor be afraid!'"

That opening was more promise than reality, for I was young and afraid. Now in my senior years, however, I see the point promised by the poem's more apt conclusion. I pause to summon the words of the poem's good rabbi, who, at a similar point in his pilgrimage, gave thanks for a journey that far surpassed any he might have ever dreamed or imagined and offered up its final product to the great Creator.

So take and use Thy work:
Amend what flaws may lurk,
What strain o' the stuff, what warpings past the aim!
My times be in Thy hand!
Perfect the cup as planned!
Let age approve of youth, and death complete the
same!

Chapter 8

Eulogy

AS ORDAINED MINISTER I was called on to officiate for the memorial services of all of my siblings except Franklin when a research leave abroad made it impossible to attend. The following tribute was offered for Soul Mate Sister, Wanda Davis (1933—2016) at the Russell Methodist Church.*

We are here to mourn our loss of Wanda Davis (January 10, 1933 to December 16, 2016) and give thanks for her life and the good that she so unpretentiously offered. Growing up just seventeen months apart on the farm nearby in the Great Depression, Wanda and I were like twins. We played together, we did household tasks together, we schemed and plotted together, and together we almost drove our mother crazy. You can easily imagine what it was like to be a tomboy growing up with four crusty older brothers. If you could have seen as did I the little girl growing up in a poor farm family in her dress stitched together from flower sacks and going barefoot from March to October, you might never have guessed she would one day put herself through college, earn a degree, teach elementary school

---

* The Russell Methodist Church from which grandma, Aunt Minnie, Uncle John, Uncle, Dad, Mom, Franklin, Beulah, Wayne, and now Wanda made their exit. The Roetzel immigrant family, Lutherans in Germany, assisted in founding.

children for thirty years, and mature as a thoughtful, dedicated, and loving servant who would earn from her peers the Teacher of the Year accolade. But from that unpromising childhood emerged a simple, straightforward, unpretentious woman of a disarming manner, full of unvarnished and untrumpeted goodness and incapable of self-pity or bitterness. Her trust in God was deep and rich but never put on display to discomfort others, and the inspiration for that trust came from an emphasis in family and church that we are to love as God first loved us. She leaves a legacy for which we rightly here give thanks and which offers an example worthy of imitation.

To call attention to her generosity, I want to visit three stories from her favorite gospel—stories that I have never heard as a part of a memorial ritual. They all come from Mark's gospel, and all deal with anonymous women whose stories shine light on beautiful features of Wanda's life.

Twenty-five percent of all of the stories of human interaction with Jesus in Mark's gospel are about women. One can easily call to mind stories about Peter's mother-in-law; Mary, the mother of James and Joses; Mary, the mother of Jesus; Mary Magdalene; Salome; and multiple other anonymous women. The anonymity may have been a feature of the lowly status of women in the culture, but perhaps it was something more. The women Mark memorialized were portrayed more favorably than the disciples. The disciples in Mark appear rather dense and clueless; they doubt, they seek favored power positions in the kingdom to come, they betray, they deny, they flee like abject cowards, and even when they get something right (like the confession that Jesus is the Christ), they get it all wrong. Many of Mark's stories about women, however, capture a laudable personality trait that transcended their anonymity, some of which I think Wanda shared.

In 7:24–34 we find a strange, puzzling story of Jesus's encounter with a foreign, alien, Syro-Phoenician woman out on the Palestinian coast. Her ethnic identity may not jump out at us moderns as so strange, but to be a Syro-Phoenician in Jesus's day to Israelites meant to be an "other" godless idol worshipper or even a subhuman creature. As a Canaanite woman, she, by nature, was an object of distrust, disdain, or even irrational contempt. She was viewed by Israelites an inferior, or a subhuman outsider. Marriage, commerce, the sharing of a meal, or social intercourse of any kind with those "others" were forbidden.

As Mark tells this story, the Jewish Jesus was in *their* territory, attempting to spend some time privately or secretly in reflection and conversation with his disciples. Then his plans go awry when a single nameless woman gets word that the healer is there and crashes his party. Prostrating herself, she desperately begged him to heal her young daughter in the clutches of an unclean, or demonic, spirit. In response to the plea of this desperate but unclean godless foreigner, Jesus says something I wish he would not have said, and it would have just had to be insulting: "Let the children first be fed, for it is not right to take the children's bread and throw it to the dogs."

To be called a dog, or *kelev* in Hebrew, in the Semitic world was profoundly insulting. The "dog" imprecation did not connote some kind of warm cuddly creature who licks your hands and welcomes you home happily when coming there from a very bad day. Dogs were scavengers who ate dung, stunk up the place, spread disease, bit children, and polluted the landscape. Once before a native non-Jewish people had been called Calebites (from Hebrew *kelev*) as a supreme insult that stuck.

The reader, I think, easily identifies with the nameless woman and understands the human temptation to respond in kind. She might understandably have stalked out of the meeting in a huff or lectured Jesus for his bigotry or could even have employed the oldest obscene gesture known in the Western world, the Roman *digitus impudicus,* which could produce brutal and violent responses. That gesture was simply our one-finger salute. Any one of those responses would have been understandable given Jesus's insult, but note the restraint of her reply: "Yes, Lord [*kurios,* or *sir*], yet even the dogs under the table eat the children's crumbs." The response was brilliant, and immediately Jesus recognized its brilliance and sensitivity. Her response totally demolished the artificial wall of separation dividing Jew from Canaanite, or Syro-Phoenician. The story had Jesus being just amazed by her response and has him say to her, "For this saying you may go your way; the demon has left your daughter." And she went home and found the child lying in bed and the demon gone. Oh, the joy! Suddenly, the old wall of separation was shattered; a centuries-old partition was removed. When faced with the life or death situation of a child walls make no sense.

This may sound like a strange story to be used to commemorate the life of Wanda, but I think it is perfect, for she spent her life reaching across walls that divide. As a young teacher in Charleston, Arkansas, she was on the 1955 faculty of the first school in Arkansas to quietly and unpretentiously integrate black and white students; it recognized that that old wall discriminated against the full humanity of both black *and* white children. That was before the fiasco at Central High School in Little Rock or the other incident near Walnut Ridge. The effort in Charleston was a total success, partly because teachers honored the superintendent's order not to speak to anyone about their plan and partly because those teachers, like good teachers elsewhere shunned the limelight and, in a quiet, unpretentious way, accepted every person as of equal worth. *And* the lesson learned was given life in the Methodist church in Charleston, of which she was a member (as was Dale Bumpers, the late senator), that brought black and white congregations together. But for Wanda, this ability to ignore or circumvent divisive walls applied to other aspects of her life. I never heard her speak disparagingly of members of other Christian denominations, Catholic, Baptist, or Church of Christ, or even of Jewish or Muslim congregants. Niece Fran, bless her, echoed this Wanda practice by saying she had never heard her Aunt Wanda denigrate another person to elevate herself. That gift she offered without pretense, sanctimony, or publication. It was just her quiet mode of being.

The Gospel of Mark speaks of two other anonymous women we do well to notice. Like the one above, one of these also crashed a party, a mealtime Jesus shared with disciples and friends on the brink of the passion. She broke into that male thing with a small urn filled with very precious ointment. She then lathered it onto Jesus's head or body, ostensibly sensing the dark week ahead and thus anointing his body for lordship or burial or both. Some practical folks in the meal circle then criticized Jesus for accepting this lavish display. The ointment could have been sold for twenty-five denarii (a year's wage in that world), and the money could have been distributed to the needy poor. But instead, Jesus noted that she did a beautiful thing, and wherever the story of his life was to be told, this story would be told *in memory of (this nameless) her.*

This story belongs with another brief remark about a poor widow who appeared to give too much. She threw her last two Roman small coins into the temple offering. Both stories highlight acts of anonymous generosity. Such generosity, I suggest, was also a feature of the life of dear Wanda. In her quiet, little, and large ways, she offered herself to the world—simply and quietly. She prepared and delivered meals to workers cleaning the Smith cemetery, who were hallowing the memory of small and great who had gone before. Unable to raise an elderly friend, she drove to the house to find her fallen and near death and sounded the alarm. She collected stones tumbled by millions of years of wave action on the North Shore of Lake Superior, one for each of her little fourth graders who were trying to make sense of the world's fascinating geology. I would guess from the stories we have heard about her in the last two days that some of those onetime fourth graders still have those stones. We could each add our examples to a long list, but there is not enough time for that; our best way to hallow her memory is hardly to make a list but to sanctify her memory by imitating her anonymous self-giving.

No one here is a stranger to the struggle she had with dementia in her waning years nor to the way she sometimes indicated that she saw death as a friend who could liberate her from that struggle, but in summary, whenever or wherever, her life story was one of freedom found in simple goodness, a story so well articulated by the nineteenth-century Quaker song set to a simple dance tune. Let us listen to its lyrics:

> 'Tis the gift to be simple, 'tis the gift to be free
> 'Tis the gift to come down where we ought to be,
> And when we find ourselves in the place just right,
> 'Twill be in the valley of love and delight.

When true simplicity is gained,
To bow and to bend we shan't be ashamed,
To turn, turn will be our delight,
Till by turning, turning we come 'round right.*

I think we would agree that she "came round right," and for that "coming round," now, let us offer our thanks.

We give thee thanks, O Lord, for the life of the one who so recently bowed and prayed with us in this place, who shared our days and nights, who brought to her world the rich experience of Christian living. We are grateful for the ways she removed walls that divide and that she did not leave the world as she found it but instead molded it, enriched it, and kept it going. We bless thee for her living example of faith, hope, and love clothed in patience and generosity. We confess the special grief each of us owns, and we acknowledge our common debt to this one for whose life we express a common gratitude. We offer this prayer in the name of him who promised comfort to all who mourn, even Jesus the Christ. Amen.

---

* This need was already sensed over a century ago by Joseph Brackett, an elder in the Shaker Church. In 1848 at 51, he believed he received both the lyrics and music by divine revelation for his "Simple Gifts." The song remained exclusively the property of the Shaker community until it appeared in Aaron Copeland's "Appalachian Spring" in 1944. Now it is one of the most popular musical pieces in America. This is a perfect portrayal of the life of the one whom we mourn and honor this day.

Chapter 9

Appendix

Images

Artifacts left behind on Native American camp site occupied hundreds of years ago. First Image: Quapaw nutcracker with nut stains, hammer center, and ax right. Second Image: On campsite on farm close to river and creek. Artifacts below include spear points, small stone bore bit, scraper, and stone knife blade.

Lutheran church (constructed 1779) in which grandma was baptized in 1865, and confirmed at 14 in 1879. Cemetery to left of building. Located in Koniglich Freist three miles from home village.

Copy of confirmation certificate for grandma noting birth date (1865) and date of confirmation (1879). Oft substituted as birth certificates.

Stone village street in Klein Machow, home village, and countryside.

Village Stream used for household and animal needs.

Great Grandma with daughter (grandma) and five siblings
landed in New York in August of 1884. One year later she
married, Franz (Frank), and in December 1886, Leo was born.
Nine years later she was widowed with four children.

Journey complete. Grandma rests beside son Leo, husband Franz, brother Richard, and three sisters, their husbands and children.

Her younger son Franz, now Frank, born in 1892 bids his new wife, Myrtle, my mom, goodbye late in 1917 or early 1918 as he leaves for combat in WWI in France.

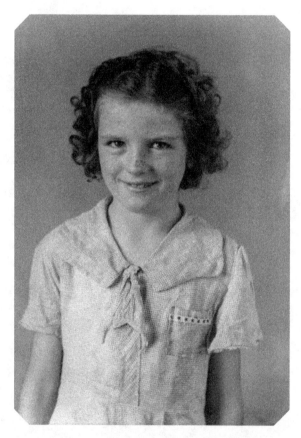

My soulmate sister, Wanda, (b. 1933) at nine
years old. The last of five living children born to
Frank and Myrtle Roetzel, dad and mom.

Mule Bud, dear friend, mentor, and protector.

Farmyard barn with wide white oak planks and shingle roof.

1937 Model A John Deere which I learned to crank and drive
when I was eleven after brothers left for duty in WW II. Belonged
to Uncle Leo who allowed us to share. Later equipped with
rubber tires. Picture courtesy of John Deere Corporation.

1943 B Model John Deere received with government permit to assist in food production for war effort. Drove home from dealer in 1943 when 12. Image courtesy of John Deere Corporation.

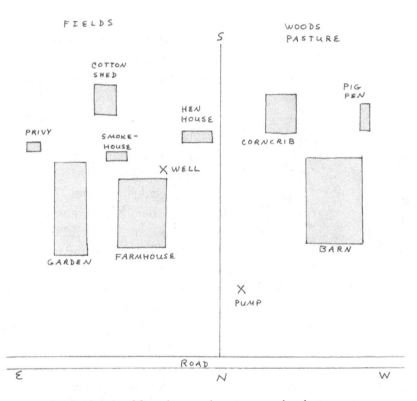

FIELDS

WOODS
PASTURE

S

COTTON
SHED

PIG
PEN

HEN
HOUSE

PRIVY

SMOKE-
HOUSE

CORNCRIB

X WELL

GARDEN

FARMHOUSE

BARN

X
PUMP

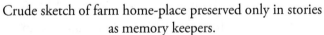

ROAD

E

N

W

Crude sketch of farm home-place preserved only in stories
as memory keepers.

About the Author

THE AUTHOR OF this work came of age in the Great Depression on an Arkansas farm, attended a one-room school, graduated from a small high school in a class of fourteen, and with the encouragement of teachers, ministers, family, and friends, went on to earn degrees from college (BA), seminary (MTh), and graduate school (PhD), be elected to Phi Beta Kappa, and to serve forty-two years as a college and university professor. He became an internationally recognized scholar of the Apostle Paul and has been called an "honest broker" of the "complex, conflictual, and evolving dynamic between Paul . . . and his churches," and his works have been called accessible to the nonspecialist, "generous, judicious, and engaged." His interests are broad. In addition to being the author of an award-winning book and a best seller, he has translated the Civil War letters of a German-speaking Union soldier, has written studies for laity, and now offers this account of how his childhood life on a hardscrabble farm during the Great Depression shaped his life and thought as an Air Force chaplain riding the DEW line, as a parish minister, and later as a teacher and scholar. At every level, he claims that the dirt under his fingernails from his Great Depression farm experience helped him understand the life-and-death concerns of common peasants in the ancient world. He freely acknowledges his debt to all who inspired his rise from poor, humble beginnings to a life of joyful service.